Drifting on a Headwind

Adventures in Remote Corners of the World

Jim Harlan

DRIFTING ON A HEADWIND

ADVENTURES IN REMOTE CORNERS OF THE WORLD

BY

JIM HARLAN

ISBN 978-0-9838372-0-6

Printed in the United States

Uncommon Adventures PRESS

UncommonAdventuresPress.com

Edited by Lynn Harlan & Ron Kenner

Cover image by Susan Pantle

Cover design and interior typography by Kirk Thomas

ABOUT THE AUTHOR

Jim Harlan is an intrepid traveler with a ceaseless passion for extensively exploring the remote corners of the world, often too extensively. An accomplished pilot and SCUBA diver, the author has traveled to more than one hundred countries over the past thirty four years of his life. The author created and owns Uncommon Adventures Dive & Adventure Travel which he has been operating successfully since 1998. The author received the coveted Conde Nast Top Travel Specialist award in both 2006 & 2007. To learn more about Uncommon Adventures Travel please visit www.uncommonadventures.com

ABJURATION

Though inspired by true events and the author's personal experiences, the following story is fictional. Any resemblance to known relatives, friends, foes, bartenders, border guards, police, smugglers, militants, governments, tribes, religions, shopkeepers, hotel owners, maids, doctors, vessels, reptiles or mammals, be they dead or alive, must be construed as coincidental despite the use of actual names.

DEDICATED TO THE KINDNESS OF STRANGERS

TABLE OF CONTENTS

OVERTURE

Like all heartbeats in East Africa, the rhythm was perfect. The bare feet of the sailors above played the wooden vessel like a kettledrum when the wind caught the sail. I had barely recovered from the month long illness in the dung hut in the Serengeti and it was all I could do to stand. The Ghanima smelled a hundred years past her prime, which, given the circumstance, seemed entirely appropriate. Sanity was no longer an option. I was haunted all night by the Khmer pit in Cambodia and the smoked mummies of New Guinea. I could not get Ian off of my mind.

As I had grown accustomed, I found Ranjit and Beech on deck screaming at each other in Swahili. The Darwinian battle of mind over matter was ongoing. My observations in Africa were that nothing survived without both. As usual Ranjit was on his game and clearly the driving force of the moment. Without doubt he had contended with last night's rum better than me. Beech wanted nothing to do with our plan but Ranjit prevailed. He knew we would be the first to dive the pass.

Jumping off of the back of the Ghanima, I knew we needed to get deep fast to avoid the strongest currents. At ninety feet I realized I was alone. Hanging onto the wall, I felt my head start to spin. Everything went black. When my vision returned I started for the surface. The moment I let go of the wall, the current caught me and I was sucked into the middle of the pass. Every few feet of ascent caused a room-spinning head rush, and I lost all orientation. I could taste the diesel in my air. Time ceased as I worked my way to the surface while the world spun beyond control.

Breaking the surface, I spit out my regulator and rolled onto my back. The seas were large so I knew I was well outside the pass. In the fresh air my mind returned long before my vision, but it must have been an hour before I realized that I was adrift. The chances of being rescued in Pemba were thin and I entered a sublime state of acceptance, beyond hope or denial. My fate was no longer in my control, and I would only survive on the kindness of strangers.

Six-foot high seas obscured the horizon, but I could tell the sun would be setting soon. I knew the birds hovering above meant trouble as the oceanic sharks would soon follow. Oceanics wander the open sea in constant search of food and are reputed to eat anything and everything passionately. My stomach clenched as they circled.

Though I had learned not to fear sharks, these predatory specimens terrified me. The sharks opted to approach from my blindside, but a kick to their heads would send them darting into the blue. I was drawing a crowd when I heard the ruckus coming out of the sun. Thirty or forty of them approaching from all directions sent the sharks deep. Protecting me like one of their own, the dolphins chased the sharks even deeper. I was unsure if this attack was conducted on my behalf or was just part of an ongoing open ocean war. I knew that surviving the night would be a miracle. I closed my eyes in bewilderment wondering how a simple trip to Baja found me here. With the darkness came resignation. I was a prisoner. My dreams seeped through my pores.

SALLY FORTH

"Two, three hundred dollars max" was my brother's closing argument for spending the winter wandering the Baja California Peninsula. I was intrigued. Having no professional or personal obligations, I saw few obstacles in our way. We had recently acquired a relatively sound automobile. It lacked some minor creature comforts, such as a front seat and a rear window, but since we were keen on adventure we easily overlooked the shortcomings of the Rambler.

I had purchased two vinyl kitchen chairs at a garage sale, both bearing a striking yellow marmalade design, and I hacksawed the legs off to bolt them to the floor of the Rambler. They were surprisingly comfortable. This, along with a trip to the bank to empty our meager accounts, was all the preparation we made.

Like most teenagers, we awoke at noon with great excitement on the first day of our journey. It was January in Northern California and the foothills lay before us, a perfect carpet of green extending as far as the eye could see. Our banter reflected our enthusiasm, and the miles clicked away. Our goal was an ambitious one since we hoped to reach the border that same day and spend our first night in Mexico.

We hit the border about ten that night, and I immediately perceived a striking difference between the two countries. First I noticed the lack of order: people wandering everywhere selling everything from cheap tequila to caged parrots. There was a peculiar mix of diesel, dust and faint hints of sewage in the air.

The Mexican officials gave us a perfunctory glance, deemed us unworthy of consideration and welcomed us to their country.

Driving took on new challenges as I instantly became aware that traffic lights here were frequently ignored. Brian, my brother, had always argued that the best hotel values, no matter where you are on the planet, were to be found near the bus station. With this understanding, we headed into the heart of Tijuana. Brimming with life, the bus station was surrounded by massive pools of gear oil and local venders selling suspicious gastronomical delights. We parked our car on a side street. As we went in search of a room I glanced over my shoulder, wondering if I would ever see the trusty Rambler again. A taco vendor referred us to the Hotel Central and advised us not to pay more than two dollars for any room in the hotel.

In the distance I could see the twenty-watt light bulb proudly lighting the entrance to the Hotel Central. We ducked under the maze of high voltage wires that spilled out of the ceiling and were met by the obviously inebriated proprietor. We advised him that we were in need of a room for the evening and negotiations began. We settled on three dollars for the night. With a classic fifty-two-tooth grin, our host pointed down the stairs, laughing uncontrollably.

We looked down the stairs into a vision of hell. Immediately the stench overwhelmed us, the piles of trash seeming to mount as we located our room. The absence of a door should have been a tip off, but nothing could have prepared us for this experience. On the dirt floor was a mattress on which at least three generations had been conceived. The second mattress was set on a bed frame, the head of the bed at least two feet higher than the foot. I glanced into the bathroom and realized that water had not flowed here in many years. The lack of a roof provided outstanding celestial viewing. But we were exhausted and as I lay down for the evening,

I took comfort that not even the staunchest vermin would inhabit this room. Rats would not be a problem tonight.

We awoke at seven in the morning to the sight of a large stream of water running through the room. We knew it could not come from the plumbing, so it had to be the morning rain. We sprinted upstairs to check out. Our proprietor was slumped over his desk, twitching, an empty liter of Presidente Brandy still clutched in his hand.

The rain brought a sense of tranquility, and Tijuana was quiet this morning. We had few plans for this journey short of Brian's wish to stop at every Cervesa Deposito on the Baja peninsula. Beer was cheaper than water and the deposit on the bottles was more than the cost of the beer itself.

Once south of Ensenada, the Baja Peninsula took on an entirely different feel as vast armies of cacti stood like soldiers guarding the rolling hills. In Cantavina we saw house-sized boulders precariously stacked atop each other as if only giants could have placed them there. The ten-year bloom in the Viscayino Desert filled the landscape with sporadic splotches of brilliant color. We rarely saw any other cars except for the occasional massive truck that occupied both lanes of the rudimentary highway, sending us drifting off the road.

We assisted an elderly man whose car had broken down, and he told us of a remote lagoon where hundreds of whales could be seen at this time of year. Brian had an outdated map, and the gentleman was kind enough to circle the region where we could find them. We continued south to the coastal town of Gurerro Negro. To our dismay Gurerro Negro was a bleak, desolate town basking in various shades of gray. We spent the night by the side of the road after arguing whether or not it would be possible to sleep in the middle of the road due to the lack of traffic. At first the silence of the desert was disconcerting, for our journey so far had been filled with noise. Absolute silence was overwhelming, leaving our senses wanting.

Nights spent on the side of the highway inevitably lead to an early rise, and this morning was to be no different. A huge, completely overloaded truck, which it seemed we could hear approaching for hours, went screaming by at a fierce speed stirring up a typhoon of desert sands. Despite this inauspicious start, Brian and I shared a feeling that this was to be a magical day. Our map did not reflect any roads to the spot the gentleman had marked, but this did not deter us. We elected to follow any path that even resembled a road and to track it to the end with the hope that it would lead to the sea.

This was an ill-fated plan. Soon the Rambler was buried up to its frame in sifting desert sands. I knew we had only one shot at extracting the car, and we were completely alone at least twenty miles from any sort of assistance. I soon realized that in hostile environments self-reliance is critical. We jacked the car up and placed everything we owned immediately under the rear wheels, all the while giggling like little boys. We revved the engine and slammed the Rambler into reverse then stood watching as our sleeping bags and the most of our clothes were shredded before our eyes. We laughed hysterically. Eventually the Rambler dug in and, in one fleeting moment, rocketed out of its sandy grave. Without further hesitation, still laughing, we continued our hunt for the lagoon. Ironically no more than two miles after reaching the highway, we spotted a hand painted sign pointing west and stating, simply, "Whales This Way."

The dirt road ended at a pier forty years past its prime. In the distance we could see dozens of whales cavorting like children in a schoolyard. We spotted a small boat tied to the pier. Not a single human being was in sight. We pried a loose plank from the pier to serve as a paddle and, feeling quite guilty, untied the small boat and began paddling out to get a closer look at these giant creatures.

The whales were not afraid of us, which took us completely by surprise. In fact, they allowed us to get directly on top of them. Our boat was dwarfed by these magnificent creatures, leaving us feeling totally vulnerable. The young calves seemed to be infatuated with us and attempted to engage us in play. The apprehensive mother whales kept steering their young away from us while being careful not to upend our boat. We drifted in the lagoon until the last light of day and reluctantly paddled back to the pier in total darkness. As we lay on the pier that night, shivering without our clothes and sleeping bags, the whales treated us to a symphony that would bring a tear to Beethoven's eye. To this day I am grateful to the kind person who left his boat tied to that pier.

It was a sparkling day in the Viscayino, and we decided to cross the peninsula to get our first glimpse of the Sea of Cortez. We were out of food and to date had not seen one grocery store and only two restaurants. The road became very rough as we drove across the foothills that define the center of the Baja Peninsula. The simple beauty of the desert captivated us. As we glimpsed the Sea of Cortez, the grandeur of Baja came fully into view. A very weathered sign pointed to the east with the name "Bahia de Los Angeles." For no particular reason, we decided to investigate.

As we approached this tiny fishing village, we wondered if there could be any place more remote. Coming to a stop in the center of town, we were immediately greeted by no fewer than twenty-five children, very excited to see us, who grabbed our hands and dragged us to meet Senor Luis.

A stately gentleman with a broad presence and an irresistible smile, Senor Luis shared the children's enthusiasm and graciously invited us into his home. His home was like all of the homes we had seen in Baja: a very simple thatched roofed adobe building with dirt floors and two rickety wooden chairs, no less, no more. With obvious pride, Senor Luis introduced at least twenty-four of his children to us. The extraordinary size of his family left me wondering just how his wife could have survived. Later that night I met a few more of his wives and realized there had been a division of labor.

As guests, we were promptly seated in the chairs and asked what had brought us to his corner of the world. This simple direct question took me by surprise, for I had actually not considered my purpose or even realized that I needed one. Perplexed, I attempted to explain that I wondered what was out there in the world that I had yet to experience. Senor Luis appeared to be bewildered by this statement.

"All you will ever see or need to see in this world is your family," he commented in broken English.

It would be many years later, on another continent, that I would come to fully understand what he meant.

Senor Luis urged us to stay for dinner and, with nowhere else to go, we politely accepted his kind offer. Near the beach was a large palapa with a multipurpose bench which served as a dining room, motor overhauling, and fish-cleaning table. We were seated here and served a generous portion of sea turtle, rice and beans. I have always admired turtles, especially sea turtles, and it felt a bit like eating a pet. Not wishing to offend my gracious host, I secretly slid small portions of my turtle dinner to the dogs who had clearly identified me as their mark for the evening. I felt a rare sense of community that evening, and left thinking that these were truly wealthy people.

The moon was full that night, the entire horizon shimmering in iridescent silver as Brian and I walked along the crescent bay. We came upon a large sea turtle struggling to make her way back to the surf after laying her eggs. Without hesitation we gently scooted her along the sand and watched her swim into the welcoming sea. I knew the dogs would be disappointed yet I hoped that Senor Luis would not cross paths with this fine lady.

After stopping to thank Senor Luis and his family for their hospitality, we continued driving south in the morning. In dire need of a shower, we'd heard that there was a hotel in Mulege that actually had one. For the past week, we had been bathing exclusively in salt water and never felt clean.

The highway now meandered along the Sea of Cortez offering striking views of the desert meeting the sea with miles and miles of untouched beaches. After wandering the desert for several days, our eyes had grown accustomed to the monotone-colored earth contrasting with the cobalt blue sea; when we first sighted Mulege on the horizon, the shades of green were startling. A true oasis lay before us and immediately we began to feel as if we were in the tropics. The sun was low in the sky and the vibrancy of life in the desert was palpable.

Mulege was a city of well swept dirt streets dotted with simple structures. There did not appear to be any electricity whatsoever. We attracted many looks from the local people as we worked our way through the chickens and goats that scavenged on Mulege's roads. With great anticipation, we pulled into the Hotel Serinidad. Not a light shone and the streets were silent, as is the way in Baja. Utter disappointment engulfed us when we realized the Serenidad was closed. Dejected, we drove to a large open area for another night's rest in the dirt. Until now we had been brushing our teeth with beer, which was surprisingly pleasant. This evening, however, we had only warm Coca Cola, which tasted somewhat like a mix of Alka Seltzer and molasses.

Despite the circumstances I slept very well that night and awakened in the early morning to the sound of a small airplane flying very low. Just as the airplane crossed the horizon it would reverse direction and return, flying equally low directly above us. After the third or fourth pass, I realized that we had parked in the middle of Mulege's runway. Quickly I awakened Brian, threw our belongings into the back seat and cleared the runway. I caught a glimpse of the airplane setting down in the rear view mirror as we continued traveling south, foregoing the opportunity to apologize.

About twenty minutes down the highway we spotted the very gentleman who had steered us in the direction of the whales back in Gurerro Negro. We stopped to emphatically thank him for his guidance. Animated by our enthusiasm, he invited us to go kayaking with him in Bahia Concepcion. We eagerly agreed and soon came upon another breathtaking stretch of coastline with dramatic sheer cliffs that disappeared suddenly into the deep. This troubled man, a master carpenter, carried two handmade kayaks of spotless construction down to the shore and then left us on our own. After several flips into the sea, Brian and I started to get the hang of staying upright in the kayaks. In total ignorance we paddled farther from shore.

The sea was flat and sunlight gleamed off the water. Then, without any warning, the ocean began to boil with hundreds of dolphins. All around us they were leaping high into the air in the purest display of joy I had ever seen. Their acrobatic maneuvers were stunning as they spun and flipped, often flying five meters into the sky. The sound was deafening with their high-pitched squeals and the percussion of hundreds of bodies belly flopping in unison. At no time did the dolphins acknowledge our presence as we witnessed their thrilling display of freedom. If I were to return to this world, I hope that I would return as a dolphin. Lost in a blue world, we paddled back toward the majestic cliffs, charmed by a perfect day.

We shared a cliff-top perch that night which inevitably led to the question of what brought us to this place. Mr. Griffin was a soft-eyed quiet man who appeared to be lost in perpetual thought. Tragically he had lost his family a year ago and seemed to be contending with this sorrow in deep reflection. We provided him a breath of fresh air with our determined spirit. It took us over an hour to get him to laugh, which I suspect was the first time he had laughed in more than a year. When we finally said goodnight, I shook his hand, looked him in the eye, and thanked him for two of the finest days I had ever spent. There is a part of me that realizes I was destined to cross paths with Mr. Griffin and that Mr. Griffin was destined to cross paths with me.

The scenery remained exquisite as we wound our way along the cliffs the next day. We stopped frequently to admire one stunning view after another. We had by now slipped into full holiday mode, enjoying each moment while anticipating what might come next. About an hour before sunset we sighted La Paz in the distance and were thrilled at the prospect of a hot shower and a real bed. As usual, we found and tracked a very large, noisy bus which led us to the station. Following a Mexican bus became true sport as a constant stream of trash flew out of the windows and inevitably bounced off of the Rambler. There was little doubt that the bus ruled the road. The La Paz bus station was relatively quiet and in short order we found a clean room with a hot shower.

Later we located a lavanderia to wash our few remaining clothes and then set out to find a taco vender. The Mexican taco wasn't anything like the tacos we were accustomed to in California. Tacos were sold only on the street and usually in suspect neighborhoods. Tiny in comparison, they were typically a mix of meat, cabbage and diabolically hot salsa. The true maestro could prepare a dozen at a time while kicking the bone-thin dog moving in from his blindside.

It was startling to see all of the commotion of a large city, for we had spent weeks in the desert with few interactions with people and almost zero sound. Brian had been speaking about visiting the Rosita since a surfer at a Cervesa Deposito in Guerro Negro had told us that many attractive young ladies could be found there. We had already learned that the best information in any town could be obtained from consulting either bartenders or taxi drivers. When we inquired about the location of the Rosita, the taxi driver smiled and pointed toward the east, well out of the city. We knew we were close when we saw that the road was blocked with a very slow moving beer truck. An architectural enigma, the Rosita was flat, square and gray.

Visiting the Rosita was a completely new experience for me, and I entered the place feeling awkward. It took a moment for my eyes to adjust to the lack of light. The first thing I noticed was the smell: a mixture of urine, sweat and cheap liquor. Frayed velvet and partially operative neon signs adorned the walls. There was no door on the restroom, which was for men only. A glance beyond the bathroom revealed twenty or so very small rooms on either side of a long hallway. The usual customers stuck to the bar like adhesive, lost somewhere between ego, guilt and sin while an antiquated jukebox bellowed atrocious Mexican ballads at distortion levels. What impressed me the most about the Rosita was the very large drain in the middle of the floor which allowed this fine establishment to be hosed down at the end of every evening. I soon realized that this was a very free place in which one could relieve himself of the Christian weight.

The ladies were young and, I assumed, desperate, for what circumstance other than desperation would drive a woman to this place. The locals at the bar appeared to share their desperation. Behind the bar stood the Mexican version of Genghis Kahn with all the geniality of a pit viper. Sitting in the dark corner behind Genghis was a sweet looking elderly lady who was there to count and collect the money. This rudimentary check and balance system led me to conclude that Latin Americans do not believe in conspiracy.

The night progressed in predictable fashion with the occasional drunk falling off his stool, the non-stop bumming of cigarettes and the hourly visits by the local authorities who physically searched all guests for weapons. By eleven the place was hopping and the music was louder and possibly even more distorted. It must have been pay day in La Paz, for the tables were full of empty bottles. The bar bill was determined by counting the empties at the end of the night, allowing the patron an opportunity to reflect on the evening's pleasures.

The women were playing the field. Since Brian and I were new arrivals, we were well received. Brian engaged the bar patrons with his high school Spanish, and I observed all the misadventures with great interest. We both held temptation in check. At Rosita's this evening there was far more talking than back room action, which I suspect might always be the case. We staggered out of the Rosita about two in the morning just as Genghis was rolling out the hose. I lusted only for the real bed at the hotel.

Having slept comfortably all night, I was extremely reluctant to depart the next morning. All roads led to a very large church which dominated the center of town. As we passed this ornate structure I recognized a patron of the Rosita draped over the church steps, twitching uncontrollably. I presumed he was seeking forgiveness for last night's sins as if redemption was entitled.

It was a quick run to Cabo San Lucas, and we were wrecked. The weather in Baja was monotonously sunny and I longed for a gray day. Cabo was a very small town with a few hotels, a campground, and a few stores. We stopped at the port to check on the ferry schedule for crossing to Puerto Vallarta. We learned that a ferry would be leaving on the following day and we secured a spot for the dusty Rambler and ourselves.

At 6 a.m. we pulled the Rambler into the hold of the giant boat and proceeded upstairs to the salon. It had a worn warehouse feel with extremely uncomfortable chairs lined up in interminable rows. We found our way to the bow. As the ship pulled out of port, we again felt that our adventure was just beginning. There are few things that stir the imagination like heading out to sea.

Having revived from our night at Rosita's, we staked out the boat for a corner that would allow us to behave like teenagers. Brian returned with some cold beers and two young ladies from Mexico City. Margarita and Maria seemed intrigued by meeting an actual American, and Brian began to play this to his favor. I was well out of the loop since my Spanish was extremely limited. I could only imagine what Brian was actually saying. The girls were giggling and whispering to each other while covering their mouths with their hands.

When the beer ran out, Margarita returned with a Bode Bag full of Baja Riesling. Wine in Baja had to be an oxymoron. It had a nose of turpentine and the effect of a charging rhinoceros. Around sundown I excused myself and curled around a few chairs in the salon. Sometime later I awoke with a Saharan dry mouth. As I was gulping water out of the ship's fountain, it dawned on me that this was a tragic mistake. Everybody knew not to drink the water in Mexico. I returned to the floor to continue suffering from my many poor decisions.

By sunrise the tragic ramifications of my indulgence surfaced. About eight in the morning, trembling with nausea, I guided the Rambler off the ferry onto the streets of Puerto Vallarta. Brian, Margarita, Maria and their considerable baggage were wedged into the back seat. I was truly hurting and went in search of a cold soda in a feeble attempt to re-hydrate. The full bottle of Fanta returned like MacArthur. I knew I was in trouble and needed sanctuary soon.

Brian was indifferent to my dilemma, for he had his sights set on Margarita. As was and is the rule of the road, I was dispensable while Brian pursued the ladies. After a very brief search for lodging, Brian settled on the Casa Lepe and secured a room at an astoundingly low rate. The Casa Lepe inspired no one. My "suite" had three walls overlooking a small courtyard showcasing perhaps twenty years of debris. The door-less bathroom across the courtyard contained a toilet that hadn't flushed in a decade. My deathbed request of Brian was a quart of milk, which he brought a few minutes later. The milk returned as quickly as had the Fanta. As I lay there moaning, Brian pulled our last forty dollars out of my pocket. The next few hours were delusional at best as I faded in and out of awareness.

In the heat of the day I became aware of a group of men shouting in the courtyard immediately in front of my room. About ten locals were wagering on a battle between a stalwart tomcat and an iguana that rivaled a small alligator in size. This was obviously a big event, for the wagers were nearing a dollar. The cat would hiss like a blown tire and the iguana would reel back with an eerie howl as the bettors screamed in ever escalating excitement. The entire scene reminded me of a bad Japanese monster movie that I had seen in my childhood. Just as the battle neared its climax, I sprinted to the bathroom startling the tomcat who shot out of the courtyard, abruptly ending the battle. As I hovered above the toilet, I could hear the men screaming at me. I was too ill to fear for my life. Soon the local gamblers realized this and started after the tomcat.

Hours later Brian returned with a smile on his face. He helped me to my feet and poured me into the Rambler, then went in search of a doctor. The heat of the day had passed, and I felt the jostling of the cobblestone streets on my spine as I lay in the back seat. Brian must have asked a dozen people where the local hospital was. He received many varied replies. Mexicans will always offer an answer whether or not they are aware of what you are seeking.

Eventually we arrived at an insignificant looking building, and the old man in front confirmed that we were indeed at the hospital. I literally crawled in the door and slumped in the corner as Brian began the negotiations for my repair. The doctor was drunk and continually grabbed at the nurses who walked past him. At a glance he determined that I was severely dehydrated. He told us that the hospital did not have any glucose and rarely bothered to stock this life-saving fluid.

Brian was dispatched across town to wake the owner of the pharmacy while I remained lying on the floor. He returned an hour later holding an old milk bottle with clear liquid. I was carried to a cot and the nurses began inserting a copper tube into my wrist. Truly phobic of all needles, I was horrified by this substantial piece of plumbing. Even though I was beyond pain, I let out a primal scream which fell on deaf ears. The nurses secured the tube with masking tape without missing a word of their constant, animated conversation.

As my body cooled internally, I felt a soothing calm creep over me. My senses slowly returned and I began to evaluate my surroundings and my current dilemma. An elderly woman lay in the cot next to me and I wondered whether or not she was alive. Suddenly and as if on cue, she began violently bucking like a rodeo bull. In the fastest action I had ever seen in this country, several nurses ran to her assistance carrying what looked like a turkey baster with a foot long needle attached to the end. One nurse immediately plunged this weapon-like instrument into her chest while three others sat on her to hold her down. I had walked out of most of the horror movies I had ever seen, but I did not have that option this time. The nurses remained sitting on her for a few minutes until she slumped back into her lifeless form.

Languishing in this hospital, I was forced to reflect on the series of poor decisions that led to my current situation. I resolved to never drink Mexican wine or water again.

Daybreak was glorious, as I was on the mend. I took great comfort when a sober doctor, actually dressed in a white coat and speaking coherent English, checked on me and announced that I would be leaving soon. Brian had spent the night on the hospital lobby floor and he looked worse than me. My bill, twelve dollars, was more than half of the money we had left. Euphoric from my recovery, I could hear every bird sing on this sunlit morning.

Puerto Vallarta was a remarkably beautiful city, and we could not help but notice the smiles on the faces of the fortunate people who lived here. Desperate people live in desperate places, and I never sensed any desperation in this jewel of a city. We wandered south to Mismaloya where there were miles of flawless beaches and very few humans. Mexico excelled at beaches with palapas where visitors could buy a kilo of perfectly prepared shrimp for a dollar. The mountains immediately behind Puerto Vallarta were lush and the sounds of parrots rarely left our ears. Life was good, and we were anxious to press on.

But we were broke, and this reality had not yet jelled. Somehow we had to scrape some money out of this country if we were to ever make it home. We pulled out the map and decided to head to San Blas some five hours to the north. San Blas was legendary with the perpetual adolescents we had met along the way, and it was about as far as we could get with the money we had remaining. The drive through the jungle was a complete contrast to the Baja scenery. Jungles reek of life, as everything appears to be thriving effortlessly. If we were to look hard, we would find abundant life in the desert, too, but in the jungle life teemed all around us.

We arrived at Matanchen Beach about an hour before sunset

and to our surprise found dozens of travelers occupying the palapas. We climbed to a small cliff to view the sunset and were greeted by dozens of large sharks circling in the shallows just below us. Unfortunately, this quelled our hopes of an evening swim to rid us of the dust of the road. Half an hour later we turned around to see a virtual ghost town. The beach full of people was now empty, leaving us feeling as if they had all been a mirage. At that very instant we began to notice a large collection of welts appearing on every extremity of our bodies. Apparently this region of Mexico was home to every biting insect in the country. Anyone in the know would evacuate the beach half an hour before sunset or be devoured by the relentless hoard of insects, most of which were invisible. We ran to the Rambler scratching nonstop and laughing.

It took another half hour driving through swamp on a dirt road before we arrived in San Blas. The number and variety of insects along the way was impressive. We had to stop several times and scrape the windshield, the carnage so thick I could not see to drive. San Blas consisted of a grid of nameless dirt roads with no apparent center. I had yet to see a town in Mexico with streetlights and San Blas was no exception. We spent that night in the Rambler parked behind a bakery.

Roosters usually have a great sense of time; however, this was not true in Mexico. At four in the morning, we were startled awake by an intrepid rooster of substantial voice who refused to be intimidated. We sat on the hood of the Rambler throwing rocks at the rooster until the sun rose. As was the norm in Mexico, this town did not immediately spring into action. Each day seemed much like the next. We decided to walk for a while to get the lay of the town.

We chanced upon the Hotel Bucanero and entered in hopes of finding a very affordable meal. In the center of the hotel was a small concrete pond filled with an enormous crocodile. A gentleman of considerable girth introduced himself as the owner of the hotel and began to tell us the story of the crocodile. Somehow this seemed appropriate. A crocodile living in the center of a hotel should come with a story.

Antonio was a warm person whom I trusted immediately. He explained that this region was home to perhaps the only swamp in all of Mexico, and therefore, home to crocodiles. It was the swamp, as well, which generated and regenerated the relentless insect population. Antonio had received the crocodile as a gift from a family member many years ago. Of course, he was only a foot long then. Antonio built a pond in the hotel and the crocodile became a fixture in San Blas. In fact, the hotel morphed into a showcase for the family pet and was a great source of pride for the family. Like most crocs, he didn't do much.

I noticed some construction had been underway at the Bucanero. It appeared to be stalled. I asked Antonio if he was looking for some help on this project. He laughed out loud and commented that I was the only American who had ever visited San Blas who was willing to work. I assured him I was serious and in need of both work and a place to stay. Antonio was impressed with my initiative and we struck a deal: room, meals and two dollars a day.

In my family I was the pragmatic one with an affinity for mechanics. Brian and my mother were scholars possessing impressive academic credentials. On a typical evening in our home, my mother and brother would discuss the fall of the Roman Empire while I repaired the toaster. I spent the bulk of my childhood tinkering in the garage with anything I could find.

Brian was due to start his second year of college in three weeks, and we both knew this was his destiny. We did not have the gas money to make it back to California. At two dollars a day, we both realized that it would be some time before we did.

In a simple act, without discussion, Brian said goodbye the next morning and began walking toward the highway. This was by far the bravest step I had ever seen any man take.

All of us come to crossroads in life and indeed this was where I was. I was too young to understand the ramifications of my situation and was at a loss to define my path. I sensed that life was just beginning.

SOLITUDE

To the local workers I was a bit of an amusement, for I had an entirely different approach to work: I actually wished to finish a project. I began to understand the Mexican mentality of non-urgency, but no one could relate to my wish to press on. Antonio realized that I was not destined to hand mix concrete, and I began to repair the wiring that suffered from decades of partial fixes and poor planning. Soon he steered me to the core problem at the Bucanero: the refrigerators and air conditioners. Word spread through San Blas that I was the gringo who could fix refrigerators, and dozens of people began courting me. I was able to negotiate ten dollars a repair. Before I knew it, I had enough money to move on.

I was excited to continue my travels. It was springtime in Mexico and everything was flowering. I stuck to the coast, passing miles of phenomenal beaches and small towns with smiling people. The ocean was very warm and I often stopped for a swim to cool off and rid myself of the dust.

Just outside of Zihuatanejo I came upon what appeared to be a refugee camp scattered along the road. I soon realized that this was the fallout of a broken down bus. The Mexican people, with their customary stoic acceptance of setbacks, began building roadside kitchens in anticipation of a bus repair that could take several days. No one appeared to be bothered by this delay and, of course, the bus was stocked with live chickens and pigs for just such an occasion.

I stopped to see if I could help. Within a few minutes, I was under the battered bus and covered in grease. The passengers appreciated my willingness to help, and they began to huddle around me to observe my random act of kindness. Almost all engine trouble in Mexico was caused by bad or watered-down fuel. In no time I had the bus running. As the engine roared, I was rewarded with applause and embraced by every mother in the crowd.

Having politely refused several offers of live chickens and empanadas, I headed for town and the always critical shower. Quite shrewd by now, I was able to find a great room on the beach with hot water for three dollars a night. I had learned to rise with the sun, which was quite contrary to my teenage clock, and this morning I was well rewarded. In the mango tree next to my room a huge flock of parrots was screeching in unison, and the entire Pacific Ocean lay before me. I took a long walk along the beach watching schools of tuna jumping in the distance. I hated to leave this enchanted town, but I had heard good things about Oaxaca and hoped to reach the city by the end of the day.

The surfers I grew up with in Santa Cruz coveted this stretch of coast and soon I began to understand why. There were rideable waves around almost every bend in the road. I had never met a true surfer who worked hard, and life in this paradise could be managed for a few dollars a day.

Feeling that all was well in the world, I pulled into the Zocolo of Oaxaca, stepped out of the car and began to stretch. Instantly a massive, very angry mob came running around the corner waving machetes, pitchforks and what appeared to be un-sanded baseball bats. Having rarely witnessed aggression in this country, I was dumbfounded by this odd behavior. I was even more astonished when the mob surrounded me screaming "death to the gringo." I ducked the first swing of a bat, but it shattered the Rambler window. Quickly I crawled under the car while furious old women tugged at my feet. Just then I heard gunshots and loud voices on a bad bullhorn. The mob scattered immediately well knowing that while guns were fairly common in Mexico, bullets were scarce.

I felt the cold metal of a rifle against my back, and I slid out from under the Rambler. There again was that fifty-two-tooth grin which I had learned not to trust, only this one had a gold tooth and wore a uniform. I was quickly swept into the back of a police truck as the mob threw rocks and bottles at me.

I was wary of police in any country, but in this case I realized that they had just saved my life. The police drove me to the local jail and threw me into a cell just as the mob began to collect outside the police station. I could not understand what the mob was shouting, but it seemed that I had committed the ultimate sin. About six Federales were pacing inside the jail refusing to look at me, which I found refreshing for the first hour. The mob outside was growing in sound and fury.

Finally the cell door opened and in walked a priest dressed in his Sunday best. Like the Federales, he never looked at me. In a low voice, he began to read me "The Last Rights." Even at my young age, I realized that everyone knows when he is guilty. This time I was not, and, for this reason, I elected not to panic. The priest never made eye contact with me, which struck me as very odd. About an hour later three Federales entered my cell and began their predictable interrogation. All three were portly and looked as if they had been drinking heavily for decades. Their uniforms were torn, their shirts were hanging out, and I could see the rust on their guns.

Over their shoulders I spotted two more Federales ripping the Rambler apart in search of evidence. Since my weak Spanish was better than their English, their ploys were ineffective. Eventually I learned that some gringo had stolen the extremely coveted Gold

Goblet from the city's main church. Apparently, I was the first gringo who fit the description. The Federales were oblivious to the fact that I had arrived in town just as the mob congregated. Right then I knew I was in for a long haul. The Federales needed to serve somebody up on a platter in order to placate the masses and to keep egg off their faces.

Mexican jails had a standard procedure of letting you rot until you finally confessed to the crime regardless of your innocence or guilt. However, this was a very civil place in which I could purchase food, liquor or a woman if I had so wished. To the Federales' credit, they never touched any of the money in my pocket.

Mexican jails also had a teenage boy who worked as the middleman in procuring almost anything I desired. My representative was a sweet kid named Luis. He would come by every few hours, smiling radiantly, and politely ask if I needed anything. Luis seemed not to place any disrespect on criminals and was thrilled to have an American in his yard. With some reluctance, he would ask questions about America in which he appeared to be endlessly interested. His mother's chicken mole, available for a small price, was the finest I had ever tasted, so I tried to keep what little money I spent in his family.

Luis was the first one to read my eyes correctly and realize my innocence. Even the indifferent Federales were starting to notice that my attitude was constantly positive and that I did not seem to possess the character of a man who would steal from the church. Truth be told, I had never even entered a church. Occasionally the Federales would throw a placebo criminal in my cell to befriend me hoping that I would divulge the location of the sacred goblet. In this game of patience, I seemed to be winning. Ten days later even the head Federale smiled at me in some sort of perverse acknowledgment of my fortitude. As usual what I missed the most was a shower, and after ten days I was ripe.

On the morning of the eleventh day, without ceremony or a single spoken word, my cell door opened and I immediately exited without acknowledging anyone. I found the Rambler in dozens of pieces scattered around the back of the police station. The key was in the ignition and everything appeared to be there. Without looking up, I stuffed all of my possessions and the strewn-about auto parts into the Rambler and drove out of town, not once checking my rear view mirror.

A few hours out of Oaxaca, I pulled into the jungle and followed the dirt road to the river where I spent an hour washing away the previous days. The Federales had removed every panel and cover from the Rambler, so I spent the following day at the river re-assembling the car. I took many breaks to swim and watch the parrots feed on the fruit of the trees that lined the river. I had hoped to continue on to Guatemala, but the locals who lived on the river warned me that it was not safe to drive through Chiapas. The people of Chiapas were successfully seceding from the reach of the Mexican Government and accomplishing this worthy feat through lawlessness.

By default I set out for the Yucatan, already forgetting the incident in Oaxaca. I have always felt the most endearing part of humanity is the ability to forget and forgive.

The Yucatan was flat, thickly forested and sweltering hot, and there was a noticeable lean toward Mayan blood in the features and behavior of the people. People of the Yucatan planted their yards with flowers. There was no perfunctory pile of refuse just outside the window. In exquisite little townships proud, well-dressed women swept the dirt in front of their homes and businesses. The Yucatan is a place with a great sense of history and the people here seemed to honor their legacy.

I had not seen a flat or straight road in months and I enjoyed the ability to let my eyes wander off of the road. I had spent months dodging cattle, children and abandoned cars seemingly always just at the apex of a blind curve. I could not relax while driving in Mexico and driving at night became almost suicidal. Despite this, I often chose to drive at night in the Yucatan since it was punishingly hot and humid during the daytime hours. The density of the jungle made this somewhat of a game as cotimundi, monkeys and snakes, who live on the roads at night, seemed oblivious to the impending doom that the Rambler would bring. Often I would be brought to a complete stop while a paralyzed creature, dazed by my headlights, attempted to determine what kind of animal I was. As always, a barrage of insects collected on the Rambler, proof that I was in primeval rainforest.

At sunrise I parked at Punta Cancun to find the most glorious beach I had ever set foot on. I had never seen sand so white or water so blue. I swam for hours chasing multi-colored fish in a turquoise world. I had seen beaches like this on posters but still found it hard to believe any place could be so beautiful. The word around town was that thousands of workers were migrating to this corner of Mexico to build the largest resort city in Mexico. As I continued south that afternoon, I thought this might be the hopeful dream of people who are tired of eating fish. I suspected that it would be many years until this region found prosperity.

An hour or so south was the impressive Mayan Ruin of Tulum, which, like everything else is this corner of the world, was set on a stunning beach. I was intrigued that the Mayan's would build such a magnificent structure so near the ocean which had a long history of hurricanes. To my surprise there were only a few people in this area and they were associated with the one-table restaurant where the road ended. I had Tulum to myself to explore every corner in peace and solitude. I spent that night on Tulum's main plaza thinking about times prior to our forefather's arrival in the Yucatan and wondered how the world must have appeared to the very first Mayan.

I followed the dirt and sand roads along the coast, occasionally asking the locals how far it was to Belize.

"By boat or by road?" they always asked me.

Many told me that there was no road to Belize. I could not fathom that any person would not be aware of all roads within a hundred miles of his or her home. I was soon to learn exactly what they meant as all roads seemed to end at the same river.

There had been a bridge sometime back, but the summer rains had washed it away and plans for new bridge were shelved. Everyone smiled and told me to try the next village up the river. To get to the next village I had to drive an hour inland and back to get a mile up river. Around the fourth village up river, I met a young boy who explained that if I were to return here tomorrow he would be able to get me and my car across the river for ten dollars. He never did bother to tell me how he was going to do this, expecting me to trust his word.

Having no choice, I returned the following morning to find many villagers awaiting my arrival. There was great enthusiasm in the air and I was treated like a celebrity. The plan was simple. The villagers had tied several mahogany logs together and I was to drive my car onto the raft, presumably cross the river and drive off. I sensed that everyone was going to share in the fortune they were charging me. Everyone wanted to be in charge.

The problem was that these logs were very thick and the river was running. Undaunted, twenty or so villagers held onto the raft while another twenty literally picked up the Rambler and set in on the rudimentary raft. At that very moment, the villagers let go and my car began to drift down the river without me or anyone else. The shouting was deafening as the villagers and I began to run along the river's edge in a state of shock.

As was the rule in the bush, the villagers were not to receive the money until my car was securely on the other side of the river, which I suspected was their primary cause for concern. We caught up with the Rambler about half a mile later as it turned a corner. Four of us leapt in the river and caught the raft. We smiled triumphantly until we realized that we were all now in the same precarious position, drifting uncontrollably down river with the Rambler.

From the rapid and animated conversation of the villagers I understood that we had to get across the river soon, since there were several large boulders down river that would destroy the raft. I immediately grabbed the rope out of the Rambler's trunk and tied it to the bumper. The villager next to me leapt off the raft at the other end and swam across the river. This kid could swim and soon he was ashore wrapping the rope around a tree and frantically trying to tie a knot before all slack disappeared. When the slack ran out, we all flew off of the raft. The rambler slammed into the opposite bank of the river and held. We all roared with victory.

Soon the remaining villagers, including the children, arrived by numerous canoes. All broke into big smiles when they saw us across the river. Perhaps one hundred of us were now sitting on the riverbank embracing our success. Once again about twenty of us picked up the Rambler and placed it on terra firma. The only dilemma remaining was how to get the Rambler to the road. Together we began hacking at the jungle with machetes. Soon we found the road and the children pushed the Rambler across the fallen brush. None of us wanted this adventure to end. I took the time to thank everyone individually for their energy. I reached into my pocket and pulled out two wet twenty-dollar bills and gave them to the kid who had negotiated the deal.

No one wanted to accept my money since we were now family.

I suggested that they throw a party for all of the children, hoping this would be acceptable to the conscience of these decent and proud people. This suggestion made everybody comfortable and a few women cried. With great reluctance I waved goodbye and drove away slowly so the children and dogs could keep chasing after me. I knew that forty dollars was a huge amount of money to these villagers. I did not have the heart to tell them that the wood in the raft would have sold for a thousand dollars in my hometown.

When I arrived at the Belize border town of Chetumal, I was told that the border was closed for "a while" for some sort of holiday. As I pried deeper, I learned that the border had been closed for four days and no one knew when it would open again. The collection of people waiting to cross the border was so small that I had to wonder if I was the only one interested in getting to Belize. By now I had learned to accept such circumstances and viewed this as an opportunity to relax for a few days.

I drove north until I found the first road heading east toward the ocean. This was about as bad a road as I had yet seen and a faded sign announced "Playa Chinchorro." Playa Chinchorro consisted of maybe a dozen houses and one very small hotel. The beach ran for miles and there were three beat-up fishing boats in front of a few palapas. Absolutely nobody was in sight, creating the feeling of a ghost town.

I pulled over at the hotel and began looking for the owner. Every door in the hotel was open and, from what I could tell, they had not had a guest for months. I left my car in front of the Hotel Playa Chinchorro and decided to go for a swim. An hour or so later I saw what appeared to be a gringo sitting on the hood of the Rambler. I swam in to investigate. At first glance he appeared to be a strong man with hard eyes that probably had seen real trouble. Rick had a Jimmy Buffet expatriate look. I was fairly sure he had spent the bulk of his life bouncing around the Caribbean enjoying the island lifestyle. The fact that he was in Playa Chinchorro meant he had doubtless burned a few bridges on other Caribbean Islands or, at the very least, he was running from the law. Rick was in need of western conversation and appeared genuinely happy to meet me.

We exchanged stories over dinner and a few beers, and I chose not to ask what circumstances brought him to Chinchorro. Rick's passion was SCUBA diving, and he offered to take me on a dive the following morning. I was truly excited about this opportunity as my infatuation with the ocean never wavered. I gladly accepted his offer.

The next morning I awoke to the sound of SCUBA tanks clanging as Rick prepared the boat for our dive. As I helped him load the boat, I was surprised at how little equipment was required to become a fish. We launched off of the beach and headed south toward Belize. A half hour later we dropped anchor at a small uninhabited island. I was expecting a diving lesson, or at least a briefing, but Rick just threw the tank on my back and put the mouthpiece in my mouth.

"Breathe normally," he said and with that he disappeared over the side of the boat.

Not wanting to appear unconfident, I jumped off the boat after him. My first few breaths defied every instinct I had ever possessed. Then an unfamiliar serenity enveloped me. Weightlessness was mesmerizing as this new world transformed me. Curiosity and the phenomenal beauty of the underwater world overtook my fears.

Fluorescent purple sponges rose out of every corner of my eye as incredibly brightly colored fish swam in the foreground. A small school of brilliant orange angelfish, their eyes bulging, stopped in front of me for a moment before swimming away. Corals the shape of a brain and sea fans of flawless symmetry swayed in the gentle current. Barrel sponges large enough to swallow me lay scattered across the bottom of the ocean, all set in a bed of white sand. In the distance I could see eagle rays seven feet across swimming in formation. The underwater world was like nothing I had ever seen, felt or imagined. I was hooked. When Rick signaled that it was time to go up, I was astonished to find out that I had been underwater for an hour. It was sure it had been no more than five minutes.

It was impossible to hide my excitement and Rick played it cool as we headed back to Playa Chinchorro. I was elated, barely realizing that it was the conquering of a primal fear that brought about my jubilation. That night Rick and I again shared a few beers and I picked his brain about the physics of diving, inquiring about locations where great diving could be found. Rick knew he had me, and he assumed the dive master role well.

Rick explained that some twenty miles east of Playa Chinchorro were the pristine reefs of Chinchorro Banks where I could find some of the finest diving in all of the Caribbean.

He added that Chinchorro Banks was a reef that was very difficult to see and that there were dozens of sunken Spanish Galleons dating back to the sixteenth century resting below water. He went on to say that there were centuries old artifacts floating in forty feet of water, saying that they were too heavy for one diver to recover. He offered to pay me twenty dollars a day to help get this booty to the boat. Diving Chinchorro Banks and recovering sunken treasure sounded irresistible, and I enthusiastically agreed to go with him. He advised that we would have to wait until Sunday to dive and, without explanation, said goodnight.

We spent the next few days rigging a simple boom from large tree branches to lift the heavy cannons he had found on his earlier exploratory dives. On Sunday a horrible storm blew in, and I was surprised when Rick said we would be leaving in an hour. We barely got off of the beach as the four-foot high waves slammed our boat mercilessly. Rick appeared confident as we began the twenty-mile crossing. The seas rose from six to eight feet, and the boat was pounding the surf and my spine. The rain was intense and visibility was poor. I could not imagine why Rick would elect to make the crossing on such a stormy day but I had to believe that he knew what he was doing.

Two hours later we entered the lagoon at Chinchorro Banks finding welcome relief within its shelter. In spite of the dark gray clouds of the raging storm, the lagoon remained indigo blue. The dolphins, like us, were weathering the storm in the lagoon and could not resist playing at the bow. Rick circled the area for half an hour and then threw the anchor in. The seas were two feet high in the lagoon, and the boat rocked incessantly as the rain pelted down. We struggled to get our gear on and as usual Rick hit the water before me. I followed without hesitation. The ocean never felt warmer as I slipped into the underwater world.

Twenty feet below the surface no one would have known that a storm raged above. Life seemed normal on the reef. As I swam after Rick, a baby dolphin, unbelievably agile and seemingly fascinated by the bubbles I exhaled, immediately engaged me. He must have circled me a dozen times in the first few minutes in pure curiosity. My nerves were shot after the crossing, and this little guy was just beginning to make me feel better when out of my blindside came what I assumed to be his mother, startling both of us into submission. She collected her baby and swam away. By necessity, I had been working on communicating without language. I knew I must be improving since I clearly understood what this dolphin's mother was telling me.

Soon, spotting Rick's bubbles, I started swimming toward him. The lagoon was amazingly beautiful with huge schools of purple fish forming a constantly moving horizon. At first glimpse the galleon seemed part of the reef. As I drew closer, it looked more like a whale carcass with its massive ribs rising from the ocean floor. This sunken ship evoked images of the era in which she sailed, momentarily displacing me back to the sixteenth century. The galleon was in amazingly good condition. I could visualize the crew jumping overboard on a day perhaps much like today. Her cannons, seriously corroded, were easily distinguishable. In all directions pottery and debris filled the sandy bottom near the ship, leaving me wondering why this wreck had not been discovered and pilfered long ago.

Rick was too busy tying rope on the cannons to acknowledge my arrival. I grabbed a rope and began to help him, observing the careful way he had tied the knots. We surfaced and began the long swim back to the boat in the pounding rain. Rick was pumped as we discussed our final plan to extract the cannons. We positioned our boat directly over the galleon and lowered the pulley into the lagoon. I was to stay above and manage the boom while Rick worked underwater. Rick dove in and surfaced a few minutes later telling me to start hoisting. The back of the boat sunk a meter lower when I felt the first cannon give way. I was sure that the boom would not hold such a load, and now that the cannon was free it was moving the boat around regardless of the wind.

Rick popped up with huge eyes and an even bigger smile. He leapt aboard the boat and we hoisted the cannon above the transom. We swung the cannon around and lowered it to the deck. We had guessed the weight to be five hundred pounds but soon discovered that it weighed much more. Just the one cannon sunk the boat very low in the water, and Rick planned on extracting all four.

It was already two in the afternoon and I knew there was only enough daylight to get one more cannon before returning home. Rick was hell bent on retrieving all four and insisted we would work through the night as he jumped back into the lagoon. At this point in my life, I knew very little about greed, but I was sure this is what it looked like. I had no idea of the value of these artifacts. They struck me as mere collectibles that might prompt an interesting story.

Soon Rick emerged and we hoisted the second cannon onto the boat. Now the back of the boat was a mere foot above water. By the time we had the second cannon settled on the boat, the storm was breaking and the sun was setting. As we rested, I asked Rick what brought him to this corner of the world. He hesitated for several minutes before replying. He told me that he had spent many of the previous years extracting people and cargo from remote islands in the Caribbean, usually at night. He got a job picking up wealthy Cubans from the beach on a quiet corner of the island and expatriating them to the Bahamas in very fast boats. One night he arrived to find the Cuban Military waiting for him. He had spent the last few years in a Cuban jail. He never did elaborate on how or why he ended up in Chinchorro, and I did not pry any further.

Now pitch black, the lagoon reflected a smooth glassy surface. Rick handed me a flashlight and explained that the first two cannons were the easy ones. We would have to struggle to free the others from the wreck below. Diving was emotionally challenging in itself, but the prospect of a night dive doubled my heart rate. Out of principal, I jumped in the water before Rick and I could hear him laugh just before splashing under.

In my haste to beat Rick into the water, I had forgotten to turn on my flashlight, so I was fumbling for the switch when I hit the sand. When I found the switch, I was astounded at how well I could see. The reef took on a ghostly appearance, and the corals were twice as colorful under the light. I immediately saw something swimming between coral heads heading straight for me. When I pointed the flashlight directly at the creature, it instantly fell to the bottom and disappeared.

I was spooked and every instinct in my body told me to head for the boat. Challenging one's fears, especially primal fears, stirs many emotions: the unavoidable one is excitement. In the microseconds that I debated my immediate return to the boat, the creature rose from the sand, staring with one alien eye. It began changing colors from green to red to black as pulsating dots ran up and down its many legs. I could only compare this encounter to a science fiction television episode that had caused me to lose several night's sleep as a child. As terrifying as this sight was, I was mesmerized.

Finally I recognized the alien as an octopus. It swam straight for me and latched onto my legs, sending me reeling backwards. I screamed loud enough to be heard back at the hotel. In a state of panic, I began to realize that this was not an attack but rather alien curiosity. I tried to keep still as my new friend explored my lower extremities, my mind racing with ideas about how I would get him off of me. We both heard a splash as Rick jumped in the water. The noise startled the octopus which let go and began to hover in front of me, proceeding to put on a display of color that rivaled any fireworks show I had seen. I took the opportunity to escape and began swimming after Rick, thinking what a bizarre encounter that was, all the while marveling at the incredible creatures which share our planet.

I caught up with Rick and had to force myself to calm down before I emptied my tank of air. Rick was carrying two metal bars to pry the cannons from the wreck, and we began to destroy the wooden mounts that held the cannon. As we attempted to pry the cannon loose, we crushed many scallops. Soon schools of fish arrived to dine on the scallops and other shellfish we had dislodged. Moments later there were hundreds of fish darting in all directions stirring up the water immediately around us and reducing our visibility to a few feet.

It was not long before the first shark showed up. Complete chaos ensued as every fish within my light scattered and all I could see was a six-foot shark chomping feverishly just in front of me. I could not tell, but I was sure I had wet my shorts and began quickly retreating for safer water. Rick grabbed my ankle and pulled me back into the fervor, laying on me those heavy eyes of a man who had spent years in a third world jail. Undaunted, he just kept thumping the shark on the head with his flashlight until the shark retreated.

Sharks feed on irregular movements and indeed everything I was doing was irregular. In no time we had a dozen sharks circling around us making it impossible for me to focus on the task at hand. I began to wonder if the twenty dollars was worth all of this. Rick had managed to free the cannon and attach the ropes. My heart sank when he signaled for me to stay as he swam toward the boat with the rope in hand. I lay motionless on the sandy bottom awaiting the tug of the rope to start the hoisting, crosschecking every emotion I possessed, watching every movement of every shark.

Seconds seemed like hours. Instead of the customary two tugs to begin the hoisting, Rick began constantly tugging on the rope with an obvious urgency. I shot to the surface. Rick grabbed my tank and pulled me on the boat. For the first time I saw fear in his eyes. He cut the rope and ran to the front of the boat.

I was stumbling to get my gear off when I saw a light coming into the lagoon about a mile away. While we had carefully entered the lagoon earlier to avoid the many coral heads, Rick now abandoned caution and thrust the boat in full throttle, lights off, and headed for the few small bits of islands at the lagoon's center. He guided the boat into a narrow mangrove and shut off the engine.

Staring straight at me, he whispered, "Don't make a sound."

About ten minutes later, we heard the sound of another boat heading in our direction. We had covered our boat with branches and shrubs to avoid detection. As we sat in silence, I could just make out the word " Policia" painted on the side of the boat as it passed by moving very slowly. As soon as the Federales were clear of us, Rick started the engine and we shot out of the mangrove heading out of the lagoon at full speed.

Instantly the Federales were hot on our trail with all lights on us. However, the Federales were not as courageous as Rick. Fortunately, they slowed to avoid the coral heads. We continued at full throttle without regard for the dangers just below the surface. Rick was in his element, noticeably excited by the thrill of the run. I began to believe that it was Rick's destiny that kept us off of the reef, offering us an advantage that mere chance would have never delivered.

The boat moved markedly slower with the weight of the cannons. As we broke out of the lagoon, the heavily laden boat began to flex with the additional stress of the waves. Every time the boat hit the surface I could feel the hull tremble and contort. Rick was still smiling from ear to ear, and I could see that he truly enjoyed the run. In the chaos of the moment, over the noise of the engine, Rick began to apologize. He was positive that the Federales would not be at Chinchorro Banks on a Sunday. From what I knew of this country, that would be a reasonable conclusion.

Back at the lagoon, as we were scattering brush over the boat, I began to realize that Rick had played me, yet somehow I knew that he was looking out for me. I assumed this was an unwritten rule in his profession. Rick continued to explain that it was illegal to even be at Chinchorro Banks, and that the Mexican Government patrolled regularly to keep divers and fishermen from pilfering the many shipwrecks before they could. He had spent many previous Sundays searching Chinchorro Banks for sunken treasure without being detected.

I could see the Federales a mile behind us, and they were slowly gaining. An hour passed in moments and I was puzzled when I sighted the few dim lights of Playa Chinchorro. Even my non-criminal mind knew it was not smart to return to Playa Chinchorro. The Federales would surely find us in this tiny village. About mile offshore Rick stuffed some cash in my shirt pocket.

"Jump when I tell you," he said with a stern look,

I hurried to the back of the boat, climbed on top of the cannons, and with a last glance at Rick, leapt off on the boat. I could hear Rick laughing as I bounced across the surface like a rag doll. In Rick's world, we had said a proper goodbye.

The blood was ringing in my ears as I floated in silence. I began the long swim to shore occasionally looking south, hoping that Rick would reach Belize before the Federales. An hour later I stumbled onto the beach, made my way to the hotel, quickly collected my things, and slipped out of town observed only by a pack of dogs. It was a pitch-black night and I was more than ready to turn the page on the Mexico chapter of my life. I was certain that luck was the only factor allowing me to continue on my travels, and I knew that I had played all of my cards in this country.

Borders with No Exits

At sunrise, without fanfare, I crossed into Chetumal, wondering what distinguished one country from the next. The Belizean officials were kind and genuinely welcomed me to their country. I was never able to find a corner of Mexico where somebody did not eventually appear. In stark contrast, Belize offered total solitude. In need of rest and resolve, I retreated to the forest. I spent several days in the bush washing my clothes and collecting my thoughts. As a western man, I found refuge in maintenance, and I took time to oil everything. In the simple act of crossing another border, I was never to look back.

Tiring of jungle fruit, I set out for Belize City on a rainy morning. The roads were deplorable and the pace agonizingly slow. I rarely saw another car or person. The jungle road was lined with exotic birds. I had become particularly fond of toucans, and I must have seen a hundred of them on that rainy day. I learned that I could estimate the population of any region by the number of birds that perched by the side of the road.

At first glance Belize City seemed like a movie set. There were shanty houses built on poles, very few lights and minimal signs of life. Few people roamed the streets and there was no traffic. It seemed more like a deserted village than a nation's capital. I was hungry and soon came upon a small nightclub with a meager gathering of patrons in front. The lively music that spilled from the café lured me in. A small hand-painted sign read, "Ruby's Cool Spot." I smiled and was greeted with smiles in return.

Ruby's was decorated in a multi-pastel Caribbean color scheme highlighted by dozens of black lights that transformed all the colors into fluorescent deviations. Three stools and four tables filled the tiny establishment and most everyone was of African descent. The music was upbeat and the room vibrated with energy. If I were to judge a nation by its music, I would immediately conclude that Belize dealt with its hardships straight up and embraced life day by day.

Ruby herself came over and promptly plopped down a cold beer. She looked at me and seemed to read me in an instant.

"Your dinner will be ready in a bit," she said.

This strange setting was unlike anything I had yet to experience. A tall, blond, well-lubricated Brit sat down in front of me and struck up a conversation. Simon had spent the bulk of his life extracting hardwood from the plentiful forests of Belize. Like most Brits, he had a flair for conversation. His skin was alabaster white, and he had mad dog eyes, the kind that come from spending too much time in the bush.

I had learned that the Simons of the world were valuable resources who would offer insights that might take me months to discover, and I offered to buy him a drink. I sensed that he was unwilling to share any of his history with me since he never inquired about mine. I was in need of work and Simon suggested I try the offshore islands. He informed me that there was a budding tourist industry for travelers wishing to explore the untouched beaches and barrier reefs of this area.

During our conversation, Ruby arrived with my dinner of green fried chicken, rice and beans. I was too hungry to inquire or even to care about color. Simon and I talked well into the night since both of us were in need of proper conversation. He provided the very insights I was seeking about this friendly laid-back country.

Even by daylight, Belize City was a movie set unlike any I had seen. The brightly colored buildings were simply constructed, and I could see through many walls as I walked the city. As the night before, the locals were friendly and all eyes were on my as I wandered the streets. The teenagers, fascinated by my presence in their country, were eager to help me park the Rambler while I went to the islands. After negotiating a fair parking and security deal for the Rambler, we all walked to the water to catch the supply boat to San Pedro. Simon had advised me to start in Ambergris Caye, explaining that it was a large island with several hotels under construction.

As the dock came into view, I saw the most energetic corner of this city: people, pigs, chickens and dogs scurrying in all directions as the men loaded the large deteriorating boat. I joined in and was well received. The locals exchanged lively conversation, and I could sense these people were at home on the sea.

The crossing to San Pedro was breathtaking as indigo waters surrounded us in every direction. When we arrived in San Pedro, I was surprised that there were no cars. All supplies were moved by cart. The town was as charming as one could imagine with all sand streets and a dozen small shops. A white sand beach ran the entire length of the island farther than I could see. The entire town showed up at the dock, obviously excited about the arrival of the boat and its critical supplies. In contrast to Belize City, the majority of the islanders were of Mayan descent. Word spread immediately that I was looking for work, and many people suggested that I speak with Ramon who was building a new hotel at the south edge of town.

As I set off to meet Ramon, I realized right away that I did not even need shoes in this town. All the roads were the same white sand as I found on the beach. Before reaching Ramon's I spotted a man hunched over an airplane in what looked like a field of weeds. I could see he was installing an engine in the airplane, and I went to investigate.

Larry was a Texan with a gentle nature and the demeanor of a bass player. He was well over six feet tall, spoke with a long slow drawl and was never in a hurry. I could see he needed some help and, without speaking, we began to work in unison. I had never worked on an airplane, but I could see they were by design simple and in no time we had the engine bolted in. Larry gave me a "good old boy" nod and walked off to get some beer.

The field of weeds turned out to be the island's runway and it was apparent that no one had flown into San Pedro in quite some time. Larry had been hired in Texas to come to Belize to work as a mechanic for an upstart airline, but the slow pace of Ambergris Caye did not suit him. He longed to go home but first he had to complete repairs on both airplanes. He solicited my help and offered me a good wage which I gladly accepted.

The next morning we walked to the runway through an empty town. I concluded that Belizeans were not morning people. Tropic Air's headquarters was housed in a tiny clapboard shack on the side of the runway. Larry entered and introduced me to Emil, telling him I was a licensed aircraft mechanic from California. I did not blink. Emil's massive body spilled over the arms of his chair. Larry went on, explaining that I was his new employee and adding that I would need a room and meals while we completed repairs to Emil's airplanes. To my surprise, Emil did not flinch and said he would call over to Lily's hotel. Without even a handshake, I became the newest member of the Tropic Air team and we went out to the field.

Larry was an excellent mechanic, always taking the time to do the job correctly. We spent the next ten days, often observed by a crowd, completing the installation of the new engine on the six-seat Cessna. We would break in the afternoon, and I would take long swims in the warm lagoon next to the runway before returning to Lily's for one of her exquisite meals. Occasionally the two pilots Emil had hired to fly his airplanes came by to check our progress. They were clear-eyed kids with an attitude suggesting respect for us, since their lives were in our hands. Within a short time we had one airplane completed and ready for the test flight.

Emil hired about twenty kids to cut the weeds on the runway by machete. Word about the flight spread quickly. It seemed as if the whole population of the town showed up to witness the test flight. Ramon, the younger pilot, walked around the plane playing to the crowd as if he were Charles Lindbergh. The male ego is as predictable as the rising sun, and today Ramon was at his best. A closer look into his eyes, however, revealed a scared kid who had not flown in a long time. Ramon knew that I sensed his fear. He asked if I would join him on the flight to offer my perceived expertise on the mechanical reliability of the airplane. I jumped at the opportunity.

We climbed into the airplane, displaying our mock confidence, and started the engine. As we taxied through the weeds all the children ran alongside, waving enthusiastically. When we reached the end of the runway, Ramon spun the airplane around and applied full throttle as we rolled down the runway. The airplane was powerful and in no time we were aloft, flying over the shallow lagoon. Ramon kept us low and we flew along the water's edge just in front of town.

We banked steeply and made a low pass over the runway while the people gathered below applauded. Ramon was beaming as he knew today he was "the man." We gained altitude and turned to the east out to sea. It was a glorious day and I found it difficult to differentiate the blue of the sky from the blue of the sea. I could see a group of islands to the south with miles of reef surrounding them. A few smaller islands lay just ahead with shorelines that seemed to drop forever into the sea. When Ramon banked to the left, we could see a submerged hole, perfectly round, surrounded by a shallow reef. The fishermen in the restaurant near the airfield had told me of this unusual place, and I agreed it was like nothing I had ever seen. I suspected that if the fishermen could see this blue hole from the air they would be even more impressed. Ramon yelled over the engine that this area was where I would find the best diving in Belize.

We turned back toward San Pedro and made another low pass over the runway prior to positioning for a landing. As we turned for our final approach to the runway, I could sense Ramon was tense and I gave him a confident look to work him through his jitters. He nailed his landing and was smiling from ear to ear as we shut down the Cessna in front of the crowd. We strutted toward the bar like Spanish Conquistadors. At that moment I knew two things – I was going to learn to fly and I was going to dive the area we had just flown over.

It was "standing room only" at the Holiday Hotel Bar and everyone wanted to buy me a drink. The Holiday, the only bar on the island, was normally supported by a dozen or so dedicated patrons but today everyone was here. I asked one of the fishermen who he thought could take me to the blue hole for diving. After much debate, they concluded that Claudio was the man for the job. The energy of the day took us well into the following morning, and at sunrise not a soul could be seen in the streets.

After a very long shower, I set out to find Claudio. I found him working on his boat at the north end of town. He took a good hard look at me. The others had mentioned I would be calling. Without saying a word, he handed me a beer. After the previous night's indulgence, I had little interest in the beer but took it anyway. This was not a moment to turn down an offer made in friendship.

We looked over his boat and exchanged stories for an hour

before we discussed diving the outer reef. Claudio had spent several years lobster diving in Honduras and had many nightmare stories to share. He went on to explain that we could live on the outer islands for a few days and get in many dives. His price was stiff, but I knew not to argue because my life would be in his hands. He said he would bring everything we needed and asked me to meet him back at the boat in the morning.

The next morning I awoke to an impressive storm and all I could think of was Chinchorro. When I arrived at Claudio's boat, I found it loaded to the gunnels. A fifty-five-gallon barrel of fuel occupied the center and thirty or forty SCUBA tanks were stuffed in every nook and cranny. The boat sat very low in the water and again I thought of Chinchorro. I was starting to believe that everyone in this corner of the world was an adrenalin junkie. I resolved to trust fate one more time.

Claudio was relaxed. It was clear that he had made this run before. He shook my hand for the first time, and we never did discuss the weather. His boat yawed under the load and it took forever to get up to speed. To get outside of the reef, most boatmen had to wait for the proper ocean swell before gunning the engine and bouncing outside. Claudio did not have this option. His heavily laden boat required that he run parallel to the reef until the proper swell appeared. We shot over the reef and took about two hundred gallons of water in the face.

Claudio kept the engine fully revved and we began to skip from wave to wave while the boat's hull strained in protest. I climbed to the front in a futile effort to weigh the nose down. For the next hour we pounded our way to the South East, slammed by the seas. An hour later we pulled into to the relative calm of the Turneffe Islands. Despite the inclement weather, here the water was very clear and marine life abounded. From the surface I could see eagle rays swimming below among legions of multi-colored fish.

There was no room on the boat to put on our dive gear, so we both threw the equipment over board and geared up in the water. We started the dive in the shallows surrounded by yellow striped fish. Soon we drifted over a vertical drop. The moment I hit the edge of the drop, I was gripped by a sensation of falling as if I were skydiving. We dropped straight down to one hundred and twenty feet and were met by two very large sharks. I had been told that most sharks were afraid of divers, but these two sent the hair up on the back of my neck as if I were confronting a mad dog. The sharks sensed my fear, and Claudio responded by thumping the largest shark directly on the head sending them both to the deep. At that point, I knew I was in the right hands.

Wall diving amazed me. Huge fans and sponges protruded toward the sea, offering refuge for every marine creature imaginable. In all directions the wall was crowded with life. We had to be among the very few ever to dive here since even the fish seemed to view us as aliens. I had not done much deep diving and was surprised how quickly the air disappeared from my tank. I signaled to Claudio that I was heading up, noticing he had his foot against the wall and was pulling on what looked like a small leafless tree. I floated on the surface for a few moments, digesting the experience.

Later Claudio surfaced holding many branches of the leafless tree. Once on the boat, I recognized them as black coral. I had seen this material made into jewelry in the shop in San Pedro. I asked Claudio if it was legal to harvest black coral.

"I have a license," he responded as he immediately stashed the coral under the seat.

An hour later we were pulling up to an uninhabited island with a well patinaed pier. Near the pier was an island style outhouse from which all waste dropped straight into the ocean. I resolved not to dive here. There was a beautiful stretch of white sand and the entire island was moving with thousands of hermit crabs. Everywhere booby and frigate birds fought for a berth in the few flowering trees at the island's center. No one had been to this island in a very long time. Indeed the wildlife appeared indifferent to our arrival.

This was to be home for a few days and we started unloading the tanks onto the pier to relieve the laden boat. After we got all the gear onto the pier, I noticed we had no food or bedding. Claudio merely shrugged when I mentioned this. Deciding not to press the issue, I simply prepared for another dive. Claudio put a large and well-used spear gun on the boat for our next dive. We motored to the other side of the island. From the surface I could see the wall dropping endlessly. We both jumped in and Claudio started hunting for our dinner. I had never seen spear fishing before and thought it best that I stay behind him. In a matter of minutes Claudio had shot two groupers and three lobsters with amazing precision. The wall here, equally as impressive as the last, was home to a dozen or so very large sea turtles. The turtles came close enough to touch and felt like a bottle that had washed up on the beach after a year at sea. I could not hot help but feel at one with nature in such a place.

We had no firewood, and I was not a huge fan of eating anything raw. As usual Claudio impressed me with his ability to turn nothing into something. He quickly built a fire from coconut husks and prepared a seafood feast beyond my wildest expectations. At night we had to build a perimeter of broken coral on the beach to prevent the thousands of hermit crabs from crawling over us as we slept. I cannot remember a night when I slept better.

The next morning we were to dive the mysterious Blue Hole that I had seen from the airplane. Claudio had told me it was a relatively unexciting dive, but when would I ever get the chance to dive this anomaly again. The Blue Hole looked as if visitors from space had drilled a hole some eighty feet across straight through the reef. Dropping down the vertical shaft, I felt as if I were being sucked down a straw. Compared to other dives, there was very little marine life and I wondered why fish did not live here. At about one hundred and thirty feet we noticed a large stalagmite that could have only come from a cave that once existed above sea level. Indeed this was a mysterious place,

Surfacing, we scanned the horizon and spotted two boats tied up to each other near the island. This surprised me. I was fairly sure we could spend a year here without seeing anyone else. Claudio seemed equally puzzled, even a bit concerned. By the time we were back on the boat, the other boats were speeding towards the mainland. I asked Claudio what he thought.

"They are probably smugglers from Nicaragua."

He went on to say that it might cause problems for us when we returned to town but did not elaborate, furthering my opinion of just how lawless this part of the world was.

The next two days we dove the reefs and ate lobster with utter abandon. I had started to recognize the hundreds of different fish that thrived here, and Claudio taught me their names in both Spanish and English. He offered to teach me to hunt, but I explained that these creatures were far too beautiful for me to harm. I was becoming a very competent diver and knew that the sea could offer me an escape like no other place on earth. I had no desire to kill any of its inhabitants.

The next morning we loaded the boat and began our journey home. The boat was light and we both felt like returning conquerors. Soon we could see the mainland and my thoughts again wandered toward cold beer, a hot shower and a real bed. As we tied up at the dock in front of the Holiday Hotel, many of the locals greeted us. Before we could even begin to tell our story, the crowd separated and out of nowhere police surrounded us. They were speaking rapid Spanish, and Claudio was saying nothing. To my relief, the police did not seem particularly interested in me. When the tall one grabbed me and pulled me down to the beach, I looked up to see the eyes of an old friend. The look on my face must have been utter bewilderment. Last time I saw Rick I was jumping out of his boat at midnight.

Rick was many things, but a policeman he was not. As usual he said nothing and he steered me into a ponga tied to a tree.

"When you hit Belize City, just keep moving and make it south," he said with obvious urgency. With that, he returned to the Holiday dock.

The ponga came to life and began heading to the outside. At this point I did not even look to see who was driving. I kept my eyes on the horizon pondering what was real and what was never meant to be. The boat sped through the waters. An hour later I could see the dock where this chapter had begun. The moment we came to stop, I leapt out of the boat and started walking in search of the Rambler. Again I knew that somehow Rick had covered me, but I did not know how or why.

NO WAY OUT

The Rambler was parked just where I had left it with the key in the ignition. I remember thinking that if this had been America, my car might not have been there. It was dusk when I started the engine and drove out of town. I would have loved to thank the caretakers of the Rambler, but my instincts told me to keep moving. I headed west toward Guatemala because there were few roads in Belize that ran south. Soon it was too dark to recognize the craters in the road and I pulled off in the jungle to get some sleep.

The next morning I awoke to the primal screeching of howler monkeys. There was never the option of sleeping past sunrise in the rainforest, the sounds being far too captivating to ignore. At the last gas station where I stopped, a young kid warned that the road to Guatemala may or may not be open due to heavy rains. I had no choice. I pressed on.

Western Belize was most impressive. Some sort of colorful bird perched on every tree, and the roads bore footprints I did not recognize. My pace, as usual, was brutally slow. I was lucky to accomplish twenty miles a day. Much to my surprise, when I stopped at the only gas station I had seen in three days I learned that I was actually in Guatemala. Everyone I met here assumed I was going to Tikal, and I was embarrassed to ask what Tikal was. People looked at me as if I had come from the moon.

"You will know when you get there," they told me.

The roads improved slightly in Guatemala and soon I started

seeing more villages and people waiting by the road for a bus that never seemed to arrive. I encountered some Americans who had been wandering through Central America for the past six months. They told me that Tikal was the greatest of all Mayan cities. It was situated in a remote jungle some fifty miles ahead. They urged me not to miss it, so I set my sights for Tikal.

Tikal made Tulum look insignificant. Set in a tropical rainforest, this was a real city with magnificent temples and towering pyramids. Tikal, even more than Tulum, seemed to be an enchanted city inhabited by enchanted people. From the top of Temple Four the view was phenomenal. Ancient spires rose above flowering trees filled with spider monkeys offering a perspective suiting the gods. The three days I had spent wandering Tikal and the forest disappeared in moments.

On the fourth day I drove into Flores to find a charming town set around a picturesque lake. Guatemalans were by far the most colorful people I had seen so far, but there was something in their demeanor that made me think of them as oppressed. They dressed in the most vivid colors one could imagine, but the personality was a shade of gray. For the first time in my travels, I heard warnings of robbers and I noticed that mothers kept a close eye on their children at all times. I was treated well by Guatemalans, but they always seemed to view me with a hint of suspicion.

I decided it would be best to drive at night, for what I knew of Latin criminals they would be drunk at night and not prone to working. For the first time in a very long time, I was driving on pavement and it was refreshing. However, along with paved roads came all the other risks I had forgotten about. Goats, chickens, AND children came darting out of nowhere and in no time I was sitting up aware of the responsibility of my actions. There were no road signs so I found myself perpetually asking directions, placing myself at the mercy of strangers. I soon learned that women were less inclined to intentionally steer me in the wrong direction. There were no maps.

Guatemala City was staggeringly large. I had been in the bush so long I was not prepared for the mass of the city, my eyes darting in every direction as I tried to absorb all the sensory input. Finally I had to pull the car over and sit still for an hour to collect my thoughts. The smell of this city was distinctly unnatural, and I began to think that I might be destined to live in a rural setting the remainder of my time. That night I drove all the way to the El Salvador border. Fearing that I had lost my sense of quest, I came to the stark realization that I had no clue as to what I was seeking.

As I had come to expect, the border was closed and the usual suspects shrugged when I asked when it opened. I knew it was futile to press, so I sat and waited for the morning. When morning arrived, I pulled up to find that the Guatemalan border guards had little sense of humor. They immediately asked why my passport did not show entry into their country.

"I have driven from Belize," I explained. They just laughed.

They hauled me into the back room and started to tear the Rambler apart assuming that, with such an inconceivable story, I must be running something. In the back room they told me that no one had ever driven from Belize before, and they pressed me for the "real story." I asked them why there was no border station between Belize and Guatemala. They simply stared back at me. Right then I began to understand that these guys had no idea where Belize actually was. I suspected they were in a position of authority due to family ties in a corrupt country. I started to posture myself differently.

"How could such a great country as Guatemala not have border stations at all points of entry?" I asked. "How could I enter this country without the government being aware? Surely Guatemala can control its borders."

I was just getting started when the border guards stood up and glared at me with rage. Passionately, they began to assure me that Guatemala was a highly developed nation, steeped in pride and history, adding that I, an American, could not begin to appreciate such a magnificent country. With that, they threw pieces of my car in the trunk and pushed it toward the Salvadorian side of the border. From that day forward, I knew I could count on the male ego to be predictable regardless of the circumstance.

The Salvadorians had never seen such behavior from their neighbors and were openly happy to see me. Sensing that I had a unique approach, they gave me the look of a "brother in arms." They stamped my passport without hesitation and waved at me as I drove off. I felt rejuvenated, knowing that in those few hours I had learned a valuable lesson.

El Salvador, a country of rolling hills, had been mostly stripped of vegetation for the purpose of farming. Churches occupied almost every corner. I was surprised at how few people I saw in the towns. I thought the streets would be full of children, scrawny dogs, goats, and chickens. It was immediately apparent that this small country was totally lost in its religion, deferring almost all matters to larger voices. When I would stop for water or food, people would look at me as if I had a second head, mumbling to each other in barely audible tones. When I would leave, they invariably cast a blessing in my direction as if I were headed for certain demise.

Later that afternoon I understood what they had meant. Just after crossing a small mountain pass some thirty miles out of the capital of San Salvador, I was stopped by well-armed guerrillas who immediately dragged me from the car and put an automatic rifle to my head. I should have been terrified, but for some reason I started to laugh.

The man holding the gun was completely baffled by my

behavior. This was a country where all threats were met with denial and prayer for deliverance, and my reaction was a first for these guys. As the situation grew more tense, I noticed that a gray haired man in the back was also beginning to laugh. He approached me.

"Where are you from, young man?" he asked.

"America," I answered.

With that, almost one hundred men started to laugh hysterically. Even the guy with the gun relented. Now I was baffled. The old man sat me down and explained that his country was engaged in a civil war and only a fool would be traveling during this time. Moreover, telling guerillas that I was an American was certain suicide. He went on to say that they admired my honesty and bravery and would cause me no harm. The old man suggested that I head for Honduras and travel only by night. During daylight, he cautioned, I should hide myself deep in the jungle and speak to no one. He then stood up, shook my hand and told me to leave quickly before one of his men had a change of heart.

The Rambler drove away to an outburst of laughter. I knew I had been incredibly fortunate and incredibly stupid. Ten miles later I pulled into the jungle and covered the car and my tracks with tree branches. I sat there in silence, watching the butterflies, thinking how uninformed I was. A month later I learned that the United States government was funding and supplying the government of El Salvador in its fight against the guerillas. Indeed my nation was the mortal enemy of the Salvadorian guerillas who had set me free.

I waited until sunset before removing the branches from the Rambler. With great trepidation, I headed south. I knew that my luck could not hold. At night the entire country appeared to be in hiding. Occasionally I would spot groups of men sitting off of the road by a fire, their weapons slung over their shoulders. I hoped they were too drunk to notice me, but I would turn off my headlights and speed up just in case. I had no idea which road to take, and I could not find anyone to ask for directions.

Eventually I learned to stop at churches for directions. Even the fiercest of Salvadorian guerillas would not challenge the sanctity of the church. At first the people inside the church were reluctant to answer my knocks. When they finally opened the door, they appeared shocked to see me. They always gave me a blessing, as if assuming they were looking at a dead man. Never once did they ask who I was or why I was in their country.

I was a few hours from the Honduras border when the sun began to rise, so I decided to pull into the jungle for the day to avoid another encounter with the guerillas. I never did well at sleeping in the daytime, and this day was no different. I was disoriented and knew I needed to get some real sleep very soon. At midday I was awakened by the sound of gunfire. Soon I heard tanks rumbling down the highway followed by mortar shells exploding on the other side of the highway. I had no choice but to sit it out, and soon I heard voices wandering the jungle nearby.

Moments later I heard the click of a gun against the car window. I knew better than to even look up. Immediately I put my hands behind my head and stared straight ahead. The door was ripped open and again I was on the ground. Then came that all too familiar sensation of a gun barrel stuck to the back of my neck. I remained silent and motionless. Whoever he was, he was alone and I sensed that he was more scared than me. As I lay there, we seemed to be at détente when somehow he realized I was not a threat and backed off. Slowly I rolled over and stared up at the eyes of a terrified teenage Salvadoran soldier.

He seemed to be frightened by the sound of gunfire all around him. I wondered if he had fled the ongoing battle, deserting his fellow soldiers. Not being much older than this young recruit, I began to feel sorry for him and he sensed my compassion.

"What are you doing here," he asked in Spanish.

"I am trying to avoid people like you," I responded in English.

He grinned from ear to ear and dropped his gun to his side. If I had a beer I would have offered him one, but we both understood we needed to part company. He gave me one last glance and then ran deep into the forest. I recall wondering how desperate a country must be to send its children to war. The battle moved to the north, and my heart never stopped pounding.

I waited until several hours past sunset before I pulled back onto the highway. I could see where the tanks had torn up the road and where some mortar shells had landed. I assumed I was now in the government-controlled part of the country and hoped that the military indulged in the same nightly practices as the guerillas. The road was quiet as usual and I was thrilled to see a sign reading, "Honduras: forty km."

About five miles short of the border, I came around a sharp curve in the highway to find a bonfire smack in the middle of the road. About two hundred well-armed soldiers pointed their weapons at me. These guys were dead serious, and I put my hands in the air thinking I had stretched my luck as far as I could. They were not children, and they were sober which led me to believe they were the cream of the Salvadoran military. This made sense since we were so close to the border. Nobody uttered a word as I climbed out of the car, my hands behind my head. About twenty soldiers rushed to inspect the Rambler for weapons or bombs. Once the "all clear" was given, I was led to a tent just off of the highway.

Once again a gray-haired man who had the ability to look right through me was sitting behind the desk. He had all of his teeth and appeared to be very fit. I knew right away this was a man who had earned his stature and was worthy of my respect. He chose to forego the normal question of why I was here.

"Where are you going, young man," he asked in a steady, low voice.

Quickly I replied that I was advised by the guerillas to keep moving to Honduras, and I did not have the option of returning to Guatemala since I had been thrown out of the country. I could tell that he really wanted to smile but his professionalism did not permit this. Before he could fire another question, I asked his name, causing him to flinch. He hesitated and then answered, "Jorge."

It was then that I knew I would be all right. I had learned that men of his position never offer their first names to anyone except family and friends.

"How are your children?" I inquired.

"How do you know I have children?" he snapped back.

"You have the eyes of a father," I responded.

With that he stood and called for the guards in rapid Spanish. I did not move a muscle. I was led back to my car where an armed soldier sat in the passenger seat holding a large automatic weapon. He pointed the weapon forward indicating that I was to get in and drive. When we arrived at the border, the soldier stepped out of the car and I was waved through the border crossing. Once again, I did not look back. As I drove the short distance to the Honduras border, I reflected on the fact that El Salvador was currently rewriting its history and I was very fortunate not to become part of it.

To my surprise the Honduran border was open and staffed by two very drunk and poorly dressed guards. They were floored to see me drive up, acting as if no one had crossed the border in years. The guards asked why I did not have a departure stamp in my passport from El Salvador. I shrugged. The guard in the plywood shack started to pick up the phone but then placed it back down. I suspect he did not want his superiors to know how inebriated he was. I stood there whistling as if this was just another day in my life, hoping that these guards would be baffled enough to possibly let me pass. In a moment of apparent conspiracy, the guards stamped my passport and raised the pole. I could see them both scratching their heads as I drove away.

The first thing I noticed in Honduras was the trash. It was strewn about everywhere. The entire country was an ashtray and every home's trash pile lay just outside the windows. Unlike Salvador, people lived in the streets with the usual animals wandering the roads freely. The Hondurans were very happy to see me. It seemed that few strangers explored their corner of the world. Everyone wanted to know my story and everyone smiled at me. This was refreshing although very few people thought I was telling the truth. .

Toward evening I stopped at the first hotel I saw. The Encantado was anything but enchanted. Horribly decorated and poorly kept, this upholstered cesspool was well past its prime. I was thrilled to see that the hotel accepted U.S. dollars as nobody in either Guatemala or El Salvador wanted dollars. I was getting low on money and I needed work soon. Tonight, however, I was going to get a shower and a night's sleep. My host promised me that they had hot water, but I was not disillusioned to find that the Encantado never had offered hot water. Nonetheless the shower was critical and the bed, despite its turn of the century manufacturer, was wonderful.

I awoke in the late morning feeling much more civilized than I had in days. I walked out front and discovered, to my surprise, that I was a bit of a celebrity. These Hondurans had not met many Americans. I assumed they thought me a mercenary, but soon realized I was just a novelty. Every movement I made was keenly observed. I asked at the hotel desk if they had any work and received the usual shocked stare. Soon I was repairing every major appliance within twenty miles of the Encantado.

I spent the next week working and playing soccer with the kids who took great joy in the fact that they were much better at the sport than I was. This proved to be a great way to make friends and the townspeople would gather to watch me flounder in the dirt. I waited until Sunday to cross into Nicaragua since I now knew that the least formidable border guards always drew the Sunday duty. I was informed that yet another civil war was brewing in Nicaragua, and my new friends in Honduras passionately warned me to not travel through Nicaragua. Accurate news was impossible to find and I assumed that the word on the streets was embellished. My instincts kept me looking south, so again I pressed on.

I was well versed in border crossings by now and I arrived at the border prepared. As expected, two border guards greeted me with a look of bemusement as no one crossed the border, especially an American. I said nothing and looked them both square in the eyes. Minutes passed while these two vacant-eyed cousins of a diplomat tried to form a question. I gestured that they should stamp my passport and then smiled. They started to laugh, looked at each other and then in unison shrugged their shoulders and stamped my passport. This was the only border crossing I had ever made without uttering a single word.

It was night and I wanted to make time so I drove fairly fast, allowing the occasional wandering pig the opportunity to take me out. The roads were quiet as I suspected would be the case on Sunday. I saw no signs of war. Sticking to my plan, I pulled deep into the forest at the first sign of light and fell asleep. I awoke around noon to the sounds of screeching monkeys. It was an unbearably hot afternoon. The Nicaraguan rainforest was dense with foliage and pulsing with wildlife. I felt as if I were deep in the jungle. All about me was alive, alert, and in motion. It was far too hot to sleep, so I began to wander the forest. Troops of spider monkeys executed their death defying leaps in the treetops and brilliant crimson toucanettes fluttered through the trees. Cobalt blue butterflies filled the sky in a dizzying pattern, and leaf cutter ants trailed off in all directions. I was invigorated. I found a fallen tree and sat there for the rest of the day, becoming addicted by the numbers and forms of life that occupied this forest. It was one of the finest afternoons I had ever spent.

At sunset I drove back onto the highway and was shocked to find a fairly large city a few miles down the road. With all the life in the forest, I thought I was hundreds of miles from the nearest city. I pulled into the gas station and found no one around. All the lights were on, but not a soul to be found. I was walking toward the office when I saw three people lying down on the floor frantically waving me in. As I entered the office, a stranger yanked me to the floor. I heard gunshots fly over my head.

About a dozen Sandinistas were barricaded behind the gas station and I could see about thirty government troops across the street hiding behind cars. I lay on the floor thinking how ignorant I was not to have noticed that the streets were empty and that I was standing in the midst of a battle. I concluded that I must have been mesmerized by my earlier wanderings in the rainforest. The battle raged on and I remained lying on the floor with my newly found friends. These guys were not scared but rather resigned to their destiny, and in this I took great comfort. I popped my head up once to see two bullet holes in the Rambler, again thinking how foolish I had been.

A flurry of bullets flew over us and then the battle moved down the street. We continued to lie on the floor wondering which one of us would be the first to stand up and dust off. I took the opportunity and peered around the corner of the building to see dark figures and fire blasting from the gun barrels. I gave my friends the "thank you, we almost died together" look and then jumped in the Rambler and tore off in the other direction. I was surprised that I was cool and began to wonder if I was ever going to recover from this adventure with my emotional foundation intact. My theory about traveling at night had literally been shot down, so I checked into a small hotel and took a long shower. The hotel owner never did look at me.

The Rambler looked good with bullet holes. They offered a patina that the car otherwise was lacking. However, I knew the recent addition to its surface would raise eyebrows at the borders and place me in a new category of traveler. I finally found a newspaper and from what I could ascertain, the entire country (in fact the entire region) was at war. I figured that regardless of any tactics, I was at the mercy of fate, so I continued south in broad daylight.

I felt innocent driving in the sunlight. Children waved and dogs barked at the passing of the Rambler. The occasional bullet-strafed building was the only sign of war I noticed this morning. A huge earthquake had struck this area, and I saw many fallen buildings. As I neared Managua, I was shocked to see the devastation. Ten story buildings were reduced to piles of dust and metal as if they had been blown apart. People picked through the piles, hoping to find something of value. I now understood why we had building codes in America.

I could see that Managua was once a great city with at least the pretense of affluence. As a traveler, I did not have to look far in Central America to see that very few people had all the money, leaving the rest to scratch out an existence. Nicaragua stood out as a country of stark haves and have-nots. This city took no notice of me. I had not been anonymous in a long time, and I enjoyed the freedom.

I had heard that Costa Rica would offer sanctuary from

conflicts, and I was more than ready to stop searching every corner for signs of trouble. South of Managua the highway followed the enormous Lake Nicaragua and soon abundant wildlife came into view. With the car window down, I could hear the screeches of the monkeys mixing with Santana playing on the tape deck. Flocks of parrots and the occasional macaw kept my eyes wandering toward the trees. Nicaraguans were friendly people and always made the effort to wave as I passed by. Given a better time in this country's history, I would have spent much more time exploring.

I stopped before sunset to check the engine oil and make sure I was ready to cross into Costa Rica. I had learned that mental preparation was a key element in border crossings and confidence was my strongest tool for quick entry. As if in a movie, the sky filled with parrots just as the sun slipped below the horizon, and I knew I was heading for better times.

BLACKWATER

In stark contrast to my previous three crossings the Costa Rican border was well built, well lit and well run. The guards appeared incorruptible and there were no visible signs of weapons. Each had all his teeth, and I noticed a stack of well-read newspapers on the desk. I immediately felt at home and was not surprised to discover that they spoke fluent English. I took the western approach and offered a passive handshake and solid eye contact, all of which was well received. Without comment, they stoically circled the Rambler. I could see they were dying to ask about my circumstance or comment on the bullet holes in the Rambler, but they demonstrated the restraint of the Queen's Guards.

These were civilized people and I suspected that Costa Rica was a civilized country. Both guards withdrew to the guardhouse, careful to shield themselves from my view. I stood perfectly still, noticing an extraordinary number of bats flying overhead. Finally, the guards returned and handed over my passport.

"Welcome to Costa Rica," they said.

I thanked them and once again found myself driving in the dark of night in an unfamiliar country.

Just as I was thinking this was too easy, I noticed a car veering onto the highway behind me. Now I was sure that this was a civilized country. A few minutes later several policemen without weapons waved me off the highway. These men did not return my smile. They searched me thoroughly before placing me in the back seat of one of the police cars. Now I was homesick.

From their tactics, I could tell they were looking for bombs. Ten minutes later a slick guy named Roberto pulled me from the car and began to interrogate me. Professionally trained in interrogation, he would start a casual conversation and then throw an "off the wall" question at me while watching for me to react. He never once asked about the bullet holes, but I could see other policemen rubbing their hands over that spot. Apparently I had evolved from a suspected drug smuggler to a gunrunner, and I did not care for my new moniker.

These guys were far too serious, but somehow I knew I would be spared the Mexican tactics of being thrown in jail and kept there until I capitulated. Roberto finally gave up and waved off his boys. I asked where I could get a cold beer and we all laughed out loud. To their credit, they never did ask about the bullet holes.

A few miles down the road I again drove the Rambler into the jungle and slept until the animals woke me at sunrise. Costa Rica was even more beautiful than Nicaragua and seemed to have even more wildlife. I was eager to explore this intriguing place, and I set out for San Jose. The abundance of road signs and the quality of construction confirmed that this was a country with a plan. Many people appeared to be of European descent, and the streets were free of trash. For the first time in recent memory I felt at home. Around every corner was a beautiful waterfall set against a backdrop of green volcanic mountains.

I had grown to expect the Rambler always to run well, so I was shocked when the engine abruptly stopped and I coasted to the side of the road. I lifted the hood and was just beginning to evaluate the problem when a truck pulled in behind me. Looking up, I saw an American with a broad smile and charmed eyes walking my way. It had been a long time since I had seen one of my fellow countrymen. Michael shook my hand, instantly identifying himself as a working man from the abrasive feel of his skin. His clothing was well worn and I sensed he had earned everything life had brought him. We both recognized the broken distributor cap and I knew I did not have to ask Michael for a ride to the next town.

We hopped in his truck and exchanged conversations as if we had known each other for many years. I had learned never to ask anyone personal questions, realizing that, given time, everyone would ultimately offer their story. Michael subscribed to this philosophy as well and our conversation was upbeat and arbitrary. I found his sharp wit exhilarating. I suspected it came from struggle, even tragedy. Some two hours later we arrived in San Jose and pulled up to his house.

His home resembled a lumberyard, and I could see he was in the midst of a large construction project. A black man, Forbes, overdressed in an outdated suit, welcomed us speaking rapidly in the Queen's English. He was a born expediter, the kind of a person who could find anything you wished. Right away he began working on me, constantly prodding for my weakness. He soon realized that kindness was my fault, and he played me like a Stradivarius. He grabbed the distributor cap from my hand.

"Twenty dollars, man," he said.

Michael gave me the nod, and I handed Forbes the money.

Michael offered me a beer, and I inquired about his project. A very well-traveled man, Michael was drawn to Costa Rica by its world class river rafting. Amazed at how few Costa Ricans had tapped the tourism potential of their country, he was in the process of building a jungle lodge on the Caribbean coast. He believed that many people would flock to the rainforests of Costa Rica. From what I had seen, I had to agree.

As we walked downtown to get some dinner, I could sense Michael's passion about what he was doing and, for that reason alone, I believed he would be successful. Soon we came upon the

Soda Palace where we were seated at his regular table. The Soda Palace, open to the city's streets, was buzzing with the voices of local people discussing politics. In stark contrast to the countries I had recently traveled through, people in this city were reading newspapers or magazines everywhere. Cuban music blared from the café and vibrated onto the streets. With the menus came a quart of Montejo rum, and in staccato Spanish the waiter inquired about my preferred mix. Michael knew everyone and was met with friendship and respect. Energy in the room ran high, and the rum flowed freely. The night disappeared and soon Michael and I staggered home, all the while discussing our perceived differences between Latins and Americans.

The next morning I woke up to the sound of city traffic, causing me to wonder where I was. I had grown accustomed to waking to the sounds of howler monkeys and macaws, and for a moment I thought I was in Tijuana. I had a pounding headache as I wandered into the front yard to find Michael already at work directing his crew. He was loading trucks with supplies for the jungle lodge project. From the collection of materials I could see it was to be of native design, which seemed appropriate for a jungle lodge.

Michael smiled and asked if I would like to go to the coast and help build his dream. Without hesitation I signed up. I headed to town to get some toothpaste and underwear before leaving for the jungle. A bland city with few architectural highlights, San Jose constantly smelled of diesel. Traffic was manageable, and it appeared that most people needed to be somewhere. Costa Ricans, well-dressed, attractive people, reminded me of Europeans. San Jose was a safe place with little crime. No one felt the need to lock their car.

When I returned to Michael's house, everybody was waiting for me, including Forbes. In obvious good spirits, he was wearing a new coat. I asked for my distributor cap, and he looked the other way. When I grew more insistent, he started talking very fast saying it would take a few more days to complete the purchase. I knew he had spent my money on his new coat, but at that moment I also realized how important that coat was to Forbes. Forbes was a man of the streets with little hope of achieving much success in the predominantly European society of Costa Rica. He took immense pride in each and everything he acquired, and I felt obliged to respect that. With this understanding, I threw Forbes another twenty dollars and asked him to please retrieve my car and park it in Michael's yard when the part came in. Forbes looked at me in total shock and smiled, knowing he had earned my trust. Again Michael gave me a nod of approval.

I jumped in one of the overloaded trucks and we set out for Tortuguerro. Once outside of San Jose, we began to climb through the strikingly beautiful mountains. I always suspected that truck drivers worked very hard, and Lino proved this beyond all doubt. He was constantly managing the truck with the focus of an airline pilot. It was slow going since the road was very steep and never straight. For the first time in recent memory, I was a passenger and I reveled in the opportunity to relax and enjoy the view.

As we gained altitude I began to see many unusual plants and birds of every color. Whole hillsides were covered with multicolored flowers, and orchids sprouted from the crevices of tropical trees. The air was cool, a sensation I had not felt in months. Soon we were near the summit, lost in a sea of gray as the clouds consumed us in an other-world experience where I could hear the sounds of life without seeing any life. This dream state was exceptional, forcing me to heighten all senses beyond vision. When we broke out of the clouds, the visual overload was staggering. I felt as if I were falling.

Soon we transitioned to tropical lowlands with miles of

impenetrable oil palms where every form of vine suffocated all light from the ground. It became unbearably hot, and I longed for the cloud forest we had just left. The road grew flat and straight, allowing Lino to relax and speak of his family. In Latin America family was everything. I had never longed for a family of my own, but the look in his eye made me understand that I was missing something. I could not dismiss this message.

We drove into the city of Limon, and I was not surprised to see life at a standstill in the stifling heat. Instantly I felt as if I were in the Caribbean since nearly everyone in Limon was of African descent. The air smelled of saltwater and spice. If I closed my eyes, I could be back in Belize. We parked in front of the American Bar and sat down for lunch. As was the custom, without request, a quart of rum arrived with the menus. The American Bar opened onto the streets and like Rositas had the flavor of desperation.

This watering hole was full of real people with real problems. Two tables away from us sat a frail looking man who was constantly hacking up massive amounts of mucous. He freely spit on the wall next to his table causing a river of phlegm to flow onto the rarely swept floor. This behavior did not raise issue with any of the many patrons at the American Bar, offering a clear insight into the clientele and perhaps Limon.

Directly across the street lay a strip of rainforest one city block square where Lino said I could find many sloths. Having never seen a sloth, I went to investigate. These completely apathetic creatures appeared filthy with their incredibly matted fur. Like most everyone else in this town, they seldom moved. Despite their obvious need for a bath, I found them cute and actually felt inclined to protect them as if they were puppies.

I returned to the restaurant and, to my surprise, my lunch was very good. We were to spend the night in the hotel just above the American Bar. With that prospect in mind, I poured myself a strong drink. Michael arrived an hour later with several members of his crew and settled in for another night of rum and music.

With sunset came relief from the heat, and the town burst into life. People did their shopping and socializing at night, and soon the streets were crowded and noisy. The characters at the bar stayed well into the night, the rum pouring like tap water. The upstairs hotel did indeed warrant my concern and I slept on top of the moth eaten blankets. We left early the next morning to meet the boats at Moin. As we departed from Limon I could not help but think that in the end I preferred real people, and indeed Limon was full of exactly that.

Moin, a tiny town set on the banks of the Tortuguerro River, had never seen so much action in any one day. Michael had arranged for a dozen long, narrow riverboats to transfer all of the building materials up the river to his building site. We spent the entire morning loading the boats, sweating rum profusely. Since I was an American like Michael, everyone who was helping us assumed I had authority and looked to me for guidance. At midday we climbed on top of the lumber and began the two-hour run up the river. The Tortuguerro River was so dead and flat I could not distinguish between the actual rainforest and its reflection on the river's surface. It seemed as if we were the first people to disturb these waters in decades. Only occasionally would we see a small hut on the riverbanks. There were no signs of humans. Large troops of spider monkeys swung from the trees along the river and we spotted many caymans sunning themselves on the riverbanks. We would startle large flocks of parrots and often glanced up at green macaws and toucans above us. Michael was right; this region would definitely appeal to tourists hoping to see wildlife.

Soon the river narrowed and the water turned pitch black, creating a haunting feeling. I could not help but wonder what monsters lurked just below the surface. Immense floating seas of grass lined the riversides and the boat's wake rippled through the grass until striking the shore. There was a prehistoric feel to this region of Costa Rica.

Arriving at a clearing, we lined the boats up against a muddy bank. No matter how exhausted we were, we still had to unload the boats before we could set up camp. We worked feverishly. It seemed every animal in the area came by to gawk at us as if we were a newly arrived circus in this small town. The daily afternoon rains came as we stood there getting drenched with our backs against the timbers. We set up camp in a clearing just off of the river, displacing dozens of reptiles and thousands of insects. Everything would remain wet for the next few weeks.

Our first project was to build a dock to offload the many shipments yet to arrive. By nine in the morning the heat became oppressive. I kept the workers motivated by example. When it was time to go into the river to set the pilings, I led the others even though I was deeply disturbed by the eerie black water. My heart raced as I recalled my recent adrenalin-filled moments in the water. This time I knew I could not see what was out there.

To the great joy of my companions, I decided the best approach would be a full on dive, hoping that my mass would scare anything in the vicinity. I could hear cries of "crazy gringo" even when I was in mid air. When my head came to the surface, I was greeted with thunderous applause. I stuck my feet into the mud and felt the river bottom squish between my toes like oatmeal. Then I glanced to my immediate left and saw a six hundred pound serpent staring directly into my eyes. I shot out of the river like a cat in a bathtub. Everyone erupted in laughter. The mighty gringo had fallen.

I turned around to see a prehistoric monster, measuring at least eight feet in length, still floating on the surface of the coffee-colored water. It appeared to be part crocodile and part dinosaur and had more teeth than personality. I had never seen anything like it. The local boys stopped laughing long enough to explain that it was an alligator gar, the largest any of them had ever seen. I joined in the laughter, and on that day we all became friends. Taking advantage of my perceived status, I dispatched the crew into the water to set the pilings. These boys knew the jungle. Before anyone stepped into a river, they first pounded the surface with a length of bamboo to scare away the monsters.

Construction in the jungle was quite different from what I had previously experienced. The wood was like steel and impossible to cut. It needed to be this way to survive the elements where wood of less density would evaporate. The workers here were skilled, and the small dock was completed just before sunset. I set up the generator and wired the lights for the camp and the dock. When the generator sprang to life, I received a perfunctory nod of respect from everyone around me. Soon the insects arrived. This was the first light to brighten the night's sky in this corner of the world and it attracted insects and animals like Mecca. If I breathed near the light, I would inhale countless insects. Equally impressive, the light drew thousands of fish to the dock. Then the sky filled with masses of fish-eating bats swarming in every direction. On occasion the bats would bounce off my head, sending pure terror to my core. I spent forty nights on that dock, always on sensory overload, never once becoming accustomed to the abundance of life swirling about me.

In the jungle, life begins at dawn. So does work in a futile attempt to beat the oppressive heat. During the required afternoon break, I chose to explore the rainforest instead of resting as I never napped well. Since the jungle was far too thick to penetrate by foot, I learned to operate the dugout riverboats. This seemed a much safer way to explore as I had heard many stories of the feared and very aggressive Fer de Lance during dinner conversations. This potent killer snake was legendary for mocking its prey in order to draw it in for the kill. More terrifying, it was prone to charging rather than retreating.

Tortuguerro is a maze of narrow waterways that seem to never end, and the jungle does its very best to swallow the water. I had to pole my way up the narrow streams, hacking the jungle growth back at times in order to find navigable waters. Huge iguanas perched on long branches over the river while howler monkeys threw sticks at me as they protested my presence. I would return to camp in the early afternoon to the surprise of my fellow workers who, I trust, believed I did not possess the skills to survive the jungle.

Among my co-workers, I was particularly drawn to a kind, apparently slow man whom I called JP. At first glance I suspected he was not "all there" due to his passive nature and his placid acceptance of his circumstances. In time I came to learn that this was his gift, and I began to admire him. A man of very few words, JP never got too excited about anything. However, when I would sit at dinner and talk about my afternoon explorations, I would catch the glint in his eye. Eventually JP suggested that we go out on the river at night since this was the best time to see most of the jungle's inhabitants. That night we set out just after sundown.

As I stepped into the boat, ducking the swarms of bats, I could feel the thousands of fish bouncing off of the thick boat bottom. My pulse raced as we untied the boat. JP had the largest flashlight I have ever seen which offered me some comfort. The sounds of the forest had never been more pronounced, and I was conscious of my rapid breathing. A mile down the river we spotted a dozen caymans floating next to the shore. Immediately we shut off the motor and slowly drifted into the middle of them. Their eyes shone brightly under our flashlight, kicking my fear level up a notch. Amazingly the caymans were indifferent to our presence and I felt like reaching out and touching them.

JP scanned the riverbank and we saw several cotimundi foraging on the forest bottom and a huge tapir rooting in the ground. As he fanned his light over the river, two narrow beams of green light reflected on the dead still water. I was shocked to see JP's reaction. He was, for the first time in my observation, very nervous.

"Fer de Lance," he mumbled as he jumped up and began pulling the rope to start the engine.

Startled by JP's panic, the caymans began to stir and a tail came over the boat and hit me in the chest. Just as in a low budget film, the motor refused to start. JP yanked feverishly on the rope. I grabbed the flashlight and to my horror saw the Fer de Lance swimming directly for us with those green eyes that haunt my soul to this day. Panic seized me and I jumped up to help JP start the engine. At the very moment I stood up, the engine sprang to life and JP threw it into gear, hurling me over the side to bounce off of what I hoped was one of the smaller caymans.

The frenzy began as I felt several caymans swipe at me with their tails. Equally as panicked, the caymans scattered in all directions. I broke the surface to see the boat moving rapidly down river and waited for the Fer de Lance to strike. Frantically I scrambled for the riverbank, but the mud was too slippery and I fell back into the water at every attempt to reach land. I was searching for a branch to pull myself out of the mud when I heard the boat returning. I think JP was still doing twenty miles an hour when, with superhuman strength, he grabbed me and pulled me into the boat as if I only weighed a pound. I landed on the bench in a crushing blow that left a bruise I would wear for the next six months.

JP raced to the camp. I jumped off of the boat and tied it up to the dock, noticing that JP would not even look at me. He climbed out of the boat, ducking the bats, and went straight to his tent. I lingered there, watching the boiling water full of fish, not even flinching when the bats bounced off my head, not bothering to swat at the insects that were devouring me.

The September rains set in, marking for now the end of the project. Everyone was eager to get back to San Jose. We had completed the restaurant, lobby and the first three rooms, and we were all exhausted. We returned to Moin filled with a strong sense of brotherhood and the pride of accomplishment. The local children wanted to touch us as we were the big news on the river that day. There were several taxis waiting for us and just climbing inside a car felt foreign to me. I was amazed to see so many people, especially women, and I looked forward to what I suspected would be an indulgent celebration for the next few days.

I decided to forego Michael's invitation to stay at his house and eagerly checked into the Amstel Hotel for my reentry into the civilized world. I showered for what seemed like hours and was genuinely surprised to see my own face in the mirror. I had not shaved for the last forty days, and I barely recognized myself. I began to wonder who I had become.

ALOFT

The rain never let up, and after several nights at the very active nightclubs in San Jose I was pondering what was next. It was nice to get back to the Rambler, and one rainy morning I decided to drive to the airport and look at the airplanes. From my early childhood, I have loved airplanes. My favorite books were about the adventures of African bush pilots, World War II aces, and the like. I wandered into the hangar of Perez Aviation and asked if they were looking for any mechanics. I was directed to Senor Perez whose office was on the second floor overlooking the operation.

The immaculately dressed Senor Perez reeked of education and sophistication. He seemed suspicious of me but soon warmed to my smile and level of conversation. He quizzed me well, but I seemed to be one step behind him, not understanding his question until well after it was asked. I explained that I had experience in airplane mechanics and was seeking work in exchange for flying lessons. Senor Perez asked why I did not need money rather than the lessons, and I told him about my recent position in Tortuguerro.

"Do you know Michael?" he asked.

I told him I knew Michael well and shared an update on his ventures. We ended the conversation by Senor Perez' saying I should return in a couple of days to discuss this further. I assumed he would be contacting Michael for more background on me.

I could not afford to live in hotels so I rented a small room just above the bus station outside of the central plaza in San Jose. I soon learned why it was so affordable. For some reason all buses in San Jose, which operated twenty four hours a day, offloaded a voluminous amount of compressed air from their brakes just after coming to a complete stop at the bus station. This deafening sound could penetrate any wall and wake the dead and the drunk.

Later in the week I went by to see Michael and he confirmed my suspicion. Senor Perez had come by asking about me. Michael was not surprised that I wanted to learn to fly since we had discussed my earlier adventures in Belize.

I had become a regular at the Soda Palace and the favorite mark of Forbes. Invariably he could be found here awaiting my arrival, eager to procure anything I might need. I chose to embrace Forbes as I could see through his hardened exterior that he was a man of immense pride and the product of struggle. One afternoon we were strolling through town without a purpose when we came upon an elderly black man, obviously destitute, sitting on the street. I was floored when I saw Forbes reach into his pocket and hand the man a dollar. This was totally out of character as he was prone to collecting not dispensing money. I waited several minutes before I had to ask. Forbes stopped and looked at me.

"Never know, man, might be your father."

I thought about this tender act for weeks. I wondered if, in his culture, everyone knew their mother but not everyone knew their father. Or was his ultimate fear that he would one day be on that street himself.

After another futile night of attempting to sleep above the bus station, I was surprised to hear a knock at my door. Standing in the rain was Senor Perez

"May I come in," he politely asked.

"Of course," I answered, wishing I had something to offer him.

He got right to the point, saying he could use a motivated

person at his organization and would be willing to offer me my suggested exchange of labor for flight time. I kept my cool and told him I would be at the airport in an hour. I closed the door and leapt in the air with pure elation. I ran to the corner, got a haircut, climbed in the Rambler and drove to the airport barely noticing the torrential rain.

Everyone at the airport was expecting me. I was warmly received by the mechanics and dismissed by the pilots. Latin America had a predictable hierarchy. In the aviation world pilots were at the top of the food chain. I knew I would have to earn my respect in this arena, so I immediately went to work as if I actually knew what I was doing. Mechanics are a consistent product regardless of culture or background, and soon I was a friend to each of them. My strong work ethic was appreciated here since no one sat around at Perez aviation, including Senor Perez.

I showed great restraint by not asking when my lessons would begin. After a week Senor Perez introduced me to Victor, explaining that he would be my instructor. I had been observing all of the pilots and I was thrilled that I drew Victor since he seemed to have the least amount of ego and a good sense of humor. Victor shook my hand, looking me in the eyes with confidence. I returned the same look and we set out for our first flight.

Victor taught me the importance of inspecting the airplane before flight, a lesson that would save my life in the future. I was surprised when he told me to get into the left seat, and we started the engine not skipping a single item from the checklist. Taxiing the airplane proved to be easy, and immediately I felt like a pilot. We were cleared onto the runway and I applied the throttle. In seconds Victor told me to pull back on the yoke and the airplane lifted off the ground. I never felt more alive. We spent that afternoon making turns over the rainforest, and I found myself torn between the miracle of flight and the beauty below. I was relieved when Victor took control for the landing. As we taxied back to the hangar, I could barely control my emotions.

We climbed out of the airplane and all of the mechanics came to greet us. They seemed to share my enthusiasm and were clearly rooting for my success. My lessons continued daily for the next few weeks, between the rains. Then the fateful day arrived when Victor allowed me to attempt my first landing. As the ground came rushing at me I had to control my instincts not to pull up early with the overwhelming sensation of impending disaster. Victor talked me through this, and before I could even comprehend space and time my wheels touched lightly on the runway and I brought the plane to a complete stop.

There are marquee moments in all of our lives and at this moment my sense of pride and accomplishment was never greater. In aviation the primary lesson is to stay calm and confident regardless of the environment. I had to bite my tongue to keep from screaming with joy.

Victor gave me a "welcome to the club" glance as I taxied back to the hangar. After tying the airplane down, we walked to the office and Victor invited me for drinks at his favorite watering hole. At this point in my travels I had not yet spent time with an affluent crowd, and I found myself somewhat uncomfortable with the people at the bar that night. The conversation was well beyond hunger and thirst and there was not even a hint of desperation. To my surprise, most of the people seemed infatuated by my presence. Finding little of substance in the crowd, my mind wandered to my next landing.

About once a week I would join one of the pilots on a flight as co-pilot. The beauty of Costa Rica never ceased to astound me, and I started to become familiar with the many small runways in this rural country. All of the pilots commented on the most dangerous airfields in the country. Invariably Sirena airstrip in Corcovado National Park was at the top of the list. Coveted as the ultimate rainforest destination in all of Costa Rica, Corcovado boasted the finest collection of plants, animals and insects in the country. When I drew co-pilot position for Sirena one morning, I was very curious to see why this region was considered most dangerous.

Of all of the pilots at Perez Aviation, I had become leery of only one: Carlos. He demonstrated too much ego in the cockpit and was habitually touting his skills. From what I had learned of flying, there was little room for ego. When Carlos showed up for the Sirena flight, I was immediately troubled. He was wearing gloves with the fingers cut off, which I accurately read as machismo. When he chose to forego the preflight inspection, I became even more concerned.

We were flying to Sirena to pick up the park rangers and an entomologist who had been studying the area for six months. As we crossed over Corcovado, I saw huge flocks of brilliant red macaws gliding over the deep green rainforest canopy. The weather was marginal. We searched up and down the coast until we spotted a tiny grass strip carved out of the tall trees. From our perspective the airfield looked impossibly short, and I could see Carlos start to tense up. At one end of the runway was a small creek some hundred meters from the beach. To add to the mix, the grass was very wet.

Since the wind was blowing from the ocean, I was startled when Carlos decided to make his approach from over the ocean. The first thing we were taught, especially on short field landings, was to land into the wind. Both ends of the runway ended abruptly in extremely tall trees, leaving us no option of aborting the landing. I noticed that Carlos was sweating profusely and at that very moment I knew we were in trouble. We clipped a tree just before the clearing and dropped the left wing. Predictably Carlos over-corrected and we stalled almost immediately. The plane dropped like a rock as Carlos futilely tried to recover. The landing gear caught the end of the creek and snapped off like a matchstick. We torpedoed down the wet runway until the left wing dropped and flipped us upside down as pieces of the broken propeller shattered the windshield. The cockpit filled with gasoline that blinded both of us. I could taste the grass of the runway in my mouth as I gasped for air.

We came to an abrupt stop. I could hear the monkeys screaming in protest. I was unable to open my eyes, but I knew that I was hanging from my seatbelt. I started to get dizzy from the fumes and the blood rushing to my brain. Fearing fire, all I knew was I needed to get out of there. I fumbled for the seatbelt and crashed onto my head still blinded by the fuel in my eyes. I could hear someone yelling numerous expletives in the Queen's English as I was pulled out of the wreckage and dragged on my face across the wet grass.

As I lay there in denial, I could hear Carlos screaming to be saved. Several minutes later my eyes stopped burning and the first thing I saw was a character out of a Dickens novel looking worse than me. Even at this chaotic moment, I could see that Ian was truly unhinged and this setting allowed him to fully embrace his insanity. His eyes darted from side to side like a man who had spent too many years in the jungle. Lacking all emotional control, he paced back and forth like a caged tiger, alternating adjectives with expletives in what I trusted was another of his many conversations with himself. I liked Ian instantly.

I sat up in a state of emotional oblivion, the kind that comes from instinctual survival. I picked the grass out of my teeth while inspecting my body for wounds. I was in surprisingly good condition and in too much shock to feel any pain. I stood up and I walked over to inspect what was left of the airplane. About fifty howler monkeys had come to look as well and were uncharacteristically silent. The airplane was totaled and I could see Carlos throwing up in the trees.

On the south side of the runway was a large open building with a tin roof, and I headed for cover as the rain began to fall. I was joined by the rangers who had not witnessed the crash. They fired off many questions in Spanish until they realized I had no idea what they were asking. Ian kept pacing in the rain, muttering to himself. We were indeed a ship of fools.

ULTIMATE TEST

Sirena Station consisted of a long open-air building simply built with local timbers and a well-rusted tin roof. Everything was perpetually damp, which I knew would include me very soon. Rangers would do six-month stints in this isolated region, and no one was more distraught about our misfortune than the two rangers with aspirations of returning to civilization. During the last two months, the rain had been ceaseless. Pools of stagnant water lay everywhere, and the insects were intense.

I went to bathe in the river to rid myself of the fuel smell. Just as the river came into view, I spotted three very large crocodiles eyeing me greedily. I attempted to scare them off by throwing rocks but the only thing I startled was a large lizard that ran across the water without its belly once getting wet. I thought to myself "I can die now since I have seen everything."

I climbed over a fallen tree and headed toward the beach for my least favorite bath of saltwater. The ocean water was very warm and I swam for an hour attempting to contend with my dilemma. I knew the only way into or out of Sirena was by airplane and nobody was going to land on the runway until the wreckage had been removed. No one could look for us until the weather improved. I knew I was in for the long haul.

Sirena Station was out of food and drinking water. We survived by eating local fruits and roots. Our drinking water came from stocks of small trees that we would cut at the base with a machete. We would then drink a cup or two of sweet water that leaked from the bottom of the cutting. Insects immediately contaminated even the freshest pail of rainwater, so this abundant supply of water was useless to us.

Ian, completely unaffected by our circumstances, spent day and night perusing his many books and perpetually searching for rare or unknown insects. I read this to be either total passion or complete absentmindedness.

In Corcovado, we had to be in our hammocks under a mosquito net before sundown or risk being devoured by insects. This made for long nights. Any bed or cot with legs would simply offer a highway for the insects. The rain constantly drumming on the tin roof was deafening but oddly comforting. I hoped I could make it until sunrise without having to go to the bathroom as a single minute outside the net carried a heavy price.

I awoke around midnight to see hundreds of bats hanging from the roof above my hammock and thousands of insects trying feverishly to penetrate my net. If even my toe touched the net, something would attempt to extract my blood. I was getting good at controlling my emotions but something told me Corcovado would be a true test.

At three in the morning I awoke, startled to the core. Something was grabbing my arm. I stared into the possessed eyes of Ian who was in his predictable maniacal state, muttering something about walking to San Jose. I calmed him down and, regardless of his lack of clarity, began to embrace his plan. I, too, had considered the inevitable reality that the best way out of Sirena was by foot and Ian knew this area better than most due to his extensive explorations.

I told him we would leave at first light. I never did go back to sleep. At dawn I spotted Ian packing a small backpack. Dreadfully short on jungle survival equipment myself, I decided to negotiate with the rangers for critical supplies. In exchange for a hammock, mosquito net, machete, tarp and fifty feet of thin rope, I offered my well maintained American car currently parked in San Jose. The rangers lit up at this proposal as most Costa Ricans coveted American cars. The deal was struck. I wrote a note to Senor Perez explaining my circumstance, directing him to give the car to the rangers.

Just before setting out, the rangers took me aside and attempted to warn me about Ian. I could barely understand their Spanish, but I clearly grasped their intent. There was genuine concern in their eyes and the only word I recognized was "loco." I was very aware that Ian was not all there, but I knew that he was also brilliant. There seems to be a fine line between brilliance and insanity. Without conversation or eye contact, we set out for Puerto Jiminez.

The only sizable town within our reach, Puerto Jimenez lay on the other side of the peninsula. I had flown there in previous weeks and knew that if we veered to the east, we would eventually find our way to this jungle outpost. Five minutes into our pilgrimage, however, I knew we were in trouble. The rainforest was barely penetrable, the canopy of trees obscuring even a glimpse of the sky. Since moss grew on all sides of the trees, maintaining a sense of direction was impossible. All we could do was follow the river and hope for the best. From the air, I had noticed that the bulk of Corcovado was flat, so at least I was not concerned about impassable river canyons.

Ian remained lost in his own world and assumed I was the leader of this expedition. Extracting comments from Ian was true sport, but I could tell he was engaged and aware of his surroundings, so I left him alone. Plant and animal life in Corcovado astounded me. Every branch held an exotic creature. The constant sounds of animal and insect life reverberated through the forest. Troops of monkeys followed along with us, accompanied by the constant squawking parrots flying above us just out of sight. Most impressive were the swarms of blue morpho butterflies that turned the world a shade of blue so lovely that I never wished to see another color.

Our progress was slow and tedious. We had been slogging most of the day and had yet to find a river. The late afternoon rains came, instantly drenching us to the bone. I had no idea what direction we were traveling, so I kept chasing the tallest trees assuming they would not be near the coast. Ian would occasionally stop to point out some unusual insects and explain the significance of the species. I listened attentively, knowing that he was on the very edge. When he spoke of his world, he was connected and focused. At all other times he was inanimate. I grew to like Ian more than ever and perceived him as a child under my care though he was thirty years my elder.

An hour or so before sunset, we tied our hammocks between trees and draped our tarps slightly above in hope of securing some protection from the rains. We had no blankets and were resigned to sleeping in our wet clothes. I slept for the first five hours, then awakened and waited the next seven hours for the sun to rise. From what I could tell Ian never slept. In the waking hours of the night, I sensed that something was watching me but dismissed this as predictable paranoia in such an environment. The following morning I noticed that several of the trees near us were stripped of their bark in long deep gouges an inch or so apart. I knew there was only one animal that could do this, and I knew that we were at her mercy.

I was eager to keep moving since we could not spend much more than a week out here before the jungle absorbed us. Ian, who was in good physical condition, never asked to rest. It seemed as if most of the animals in Corcovado had never seen humans. They stopped and stared at us, often viewing us in trepidation.

Being part of the rainforest heightens all senses. My paranoia was superceded only by my wonderment. Yet I was tiring of jungle fruits and longed for anything hot or cold.

It was the sound of a waterfall that drew us to the river. We immediately jumped in to relieve our filth and insect bites. No sooner had I surfaced when I saw the parade of crocodiles resting on the riverbank. My euphoria ended. This was the flaw in my plan as rivers in Corcovado are home to countless crocodiles. Moreover, the jungle grew down to the riverbanks forcing us to walk on slippery rocks or wade in the river itself. Our progress was more tedious than ever as we would slip and fall all the while prodding every crevice on the riverbank with long bamboo poles to see who might be lurking in the dense foliage.

Without concept of time, my awareness numbed with the intensity of this place. The river attracted all forms of life in the forest. Scarlet Macaws flocked to the fruit-laden trees, offering a deafening yet lovely chorus. Spider Monkeys executed death-defying leaps over the river, catching the smallest end twig on landing and then crashing through the jungle until they found a branch that did not snap. We were never bored. Instinctually, however, we felt that we were being constantly observed.

The crocodiles were dauntless and we soon learned that we should not encourage them to relocate as they would then slip into the black waters stopping us dead in our tracks. Black water fills the imagination with stark terror. We were better served crossing the river in a "who will blink first" competition. The crocodiles seemed to respect us and we certainly respected them. On the rare occasion that one would get too close, we would just touch its nose with the bamboo pole and it would dive into the black water.

Nightfall came quickly. Once in the hammock I spent the first hour covering my wounds with peroxide. Infections can develop overnight, and controlling them in the jungle is as critical as drinking water. Ian had not spoken in two days. We communicated almost telepathically, undoubtedly Ian's strongest method. Another week out here and I would be no different than him.

That night I was startled awake by the screams of an animal under attack. Ian was up.

"Jaguar," he whispered in a solemn, monotone voice.

For the first time I saw fear in Ian's eyes. The jaguar has a fearsome reputation in the jungle. It is the central character in nearly all the horrific tales told by jungle people. Every night the trees next to my hammock were duly marked by this animal For no particular reason, I began to call her "Cali." I determined that we were an infatuation for Cali. Otherwise she would have approached us as a threat. This was her world, and she ruled without competition.

Four days into our struggle the river merged with a large lagoon of emerald green water. These waters boiled. This was surely the epicenter of life in Corcovado, and no one had passed this way in many years. Ian explained that this was the elusive and forbidden Corcovado Lagoon and it was illegal for us to be here. I just chuckled, thinking how thrilled I would be to be arrested right now. Ian further explained that is was rumored that Castro's militia had hidden a large cache of weapons in the lagoon in the 1950s, but the exact location had yet to be determined. Many world renowned biologists had been refused access to the lagoon for this very reason. Interesting stories develop in the bush, but the effort required by any man to find the lagoon, much less carry tons of weapons, made this a tall tale in my mind.

We had to cross the lagoon and hopefully find another river draining east. I found a grove of extremely large bamboo and began chopping to build a raft. The diameter of a tea saucer, the bamboo cut surprisingly easily. It took most of the day to lash the raft. As we pushed out onto the green water I waved goodbye to

Cali, wishing her well and thanking her for not devouring us. Ian looked at me as if I were crazy.

Floating in the wide open area of the lagoon was relaxing, and I could feel the oppression of the forest canopy fall away. Any fallen tree that broke the surface was littered with turtles, and myriads of fish feasted on the many insects that neared the surface. Primal soup indeed. Otters would swim by looking as if they were considering joining us on the raft. The bottom of the lagoon was deep in silt, causing our poles to sink in the muck before catching firm ground. We circumnavigated the lagoon in search of an outlet, terrifying most of the creatures we passed. An hour before sunset, we came upon a substantial river flowing east. I had to decide whether to stop and spend the night at the lagoon or try to navigate the river by raft. The waters flowed gently, and I knew a night at the lagoon would probably tax my remaining emotional strength.

Going down river requires a leap of faith. One never knows what each bend in the river will bring. Yet floating downstream was pure pleasure compared to what we had just been through. The pace was relatively rapid and the crocodiles barely noticed us. Since the sun sets quickly near the equator, I was searching for a landing to set up the hammocks. Suddenly I heard rushing water. Within moments the raft doubled its pace and before I could even yell at Ian, we both flew into the river.

I grabbed a large rock and held on while I watched Ian disappear over a drop in the river. It was twilight and I could hear nothing except the sound of boiling water and the shrieking of parrots. I pulled myself to the bank and climbed a tree. There was no sign of Ian. I knew that searching for him was pointless and possibly suicidal, so I fumbled to set my net before the forest engulfed me. I lay awake that night feeling I had let Ian down like a parent who lost a child. I had suffered many bruises and knew I needed to get out of Corcovado soon.

In a state of delirium, I set out in the morning. I scaled the rocks alongside the river and was often forced to jump in and float with the current. I was at the edge of my emotional limits. The pressures of the journey and the loss of Ian tore at my very soul.

Eventually I saw the river drop ahead and quickly swam to the side to see what lay before me. There was Ian, sitting on a rock in the center of the river. He appeared to be catatonic, his eyes neither moving nor closing. As I climbed up next to him, he remained motionless, seeming not to notice me.

Several minutes later he said simply, "I cannot swim."

I grabbed Ian under his arms and dragged him into the river, noticing that he was bleeding badly from his left ankle. I struggled to the side and hoisted him up on the dirt. Ian mumbled incessantly and indiscernibly. Just as I was contending with the reality that we were finally in deep trouble, I spotted the skeletal heads of giant catfish rotting on the opposite shore. I knew that these fish had not leapt to their deaths and then beheaded themselves. This had to be the work of man.

The river was rapid, and I knew Ian could not make the crossing so I swam across leaving Ian propped up like a manikin. I climbed up the slippery rocks, thinking these catfish must have been eight feet long, when I saw the trail leading into the jungle. A five-minute walk led to a small partially enclosed hut with a pile of trash just behind. From the corrosion of the trash and growth of the clearing, I surmised that it had been six months since anyone had come this way.

I was thrilled, knowing that the trail would surely be our salvation. I tied my thin tarp-hanging rope to a small tree and swam back to Ian. I took hold of him and stared him in the eyes. He knew what I meant and grabbed me around the neck as we entered the water. When we hit depth, we swung downstream and the rope lost slack. Ian was choking me and I could feel him trembling. The rope was too thin to get a solid hold and it was slipping easily through my hands. I caught the knot on the end and the force of the river slammed us into the riverbank. Ian leapt off of my back and shot up the bank looking a lot like that lizard I had seen back in Sirena.

We stayed that night at the hut while I shredded my only shirt to cover Ian's wounds. We never spoke and the rains never stopped. With the morning came sunshine and hope. As we plodded down the trail, we were heartened to see clear machete scars marking the way. We wandered well away from the river, our world no longer surrounded by the sound of running water. It was steaming hot under the forest canopy. I was looking up at a sloth, wondering if they ever moved, when I heard Ian shout my name. There she was, no more than twenty feet in front of me. Her eyes were deep and hypnotizing. Neither she nor I moved a muscle. Time stopped.

Our eyes locked. My only hope was to turn my back in submission, offering the purest form of communication. As I slowly turned, I hoped Cali would not sense the change in my heart rate and read me as fodder. Ian mirrored my move, fully prepared to die. Seconds became hours and for the first time in days I heard nothing as I closed my eyes.

I was told that you would never hear the sound of a jaguar's step until she wished. The next thing I felt was her breath on the back of my knees. I slowly opened my eyes to see her passing Ian as if he were merely another jungle shrub. I took my first breath in minutes, realizing that my legs and arms were severely cramping. Still I did not move. Ian had slipped into oblivion and, without prompt, walked in front of me as if it was all in a dream. I had to follow him. He had become my responsibility, and this might be his last stand.

No more than an hour later the trail abruptly ended at the highway. We did not have the energy to celebrate or even acknowledge our good fortune. We just sat down and stared straight ahead in disbelief. We both knew that our next decision was all encompassing and would determine both our futures. We had to wonder why our paths had crossed. Ian stood up, pointed north and walked away, never once looking back.

By observing nature, I have learned that everything alive has a method of survival. I was never clear about Ian's. However, he was a survivor. I grew to respect the courage of this fine man. I knew that ultimately I needed him as much as he needed me.

YOU HAVE TO BE A FOOL TO UNDERSTAND

I heard him before I saw him. In the distance a mix of loud music and military tires came rolling down the highway, his bright red truck wide open as if he had nothing to hide. He pulled over at the first sight of me. Holding a tall drink, he gave me a look that let me know I would not have to tell him my story. He had been there himself.

A tall red-haired Irishman, Roger had the daylight in his eyes. His energy immediately perceptible, I could sense he was running. The music was pure, making me long to visit Havana. A serious drinker, he had installed several cup holders throughout his truck to secure his cocktails. When he asked me to drive, I did not question why. Despite his obvious intoxication, Roger's banter was brilliant. He was a man who had plenty of time to think.

In stark contrast to Ian, Roger was stimulating. We continued rolling down the highway exchanging philosophies while drinking rum and coke. The last thing he said before crawling into the back of the truck was "Do not cross into Panama until I wake up."

About ten miles short of the Panama border, I stopped by the side of the road and fell asleep in the front seat. The next morning Roger, startled to see me, appeared to have no idea where we were. When I told him, he became a different person as he meticulously prepared to cross into Panama. His obviously rehearsed practice, more of a mindset than a rearrangement, led me to believe that he was a professional.

The Panamanian border guards recognized Roger, greeting him warmly as he offered them cold Salvadorian beers. The slick guards performed a flawless interrogation without my even knowing it was happening. Roger spoke of women and fishing, clearly capturing the guards' interest, and in no time we were on our way. With uncharacteristic silence, Roger now took the wheel and seemed to be pondering subjects he did not want to share.

Panama was as densely forested as Costa Rica and equally beautiful. As we pulled into Panama City I was again overwhelmed with concrete and traffic. Roger parked in front of the Hotel Ideal and was welcomed by the owner, Victor. They exchanged pleasantries as if they had known each other for years. Victor never asked who I was. The Ideal was indistinguishable from the many other understated hotels I had seen, but today it was the "Top of the Mark." As usual, I longed for a real meal and a hot shower. I sat in the corner of the steaming shower for an hour. My entire waistline was covered with burrowing insects, and I hoped the heat and soap would drive them elsewhere.

Roger knocked on the bathroom door yelling "Let's go!"

At sunset the streets swarmed with Panamanians who had been avoiding the heat of the day. Spotlessly dressed police, amazingly devoid of any sweat, stood watch at every corner. Roger knew where he was going, and I joined him without question. He was at home. We got the nod from a bulldog of a man who was screening the potentials at the front door of the Ancon. We entered the squalid nightclub which was full of high energy music and loose women. Neon lights and thirty year old posters hung on the walls. This was a locals' place and most of the people seemed surprised to see us.

Predictably Roger ordered several rum and cokes, then began to harass the bartender as if he owned the place. He never spoke of the past except to recount a memorable night at a coveted nightclub in Acapulco or Salvador. He clearly enjoyed the ambience at the Ancon, his eyes gleaming as he tapped his cocktail glass in rhythm to the music. Early in the evening another American man walked into the club and sat down next to Roger. From his accent I could tell he was from the south. He was there for business. Roger was inquiring about purchasing a fishing boat. This struck me as odd. Roger had many interests and passions, but I was sure that fishing was not among them. We drank well into the night. The women loved Roger, but he seemed to prefer the chase rather than the capture. We stumbled out early in the morning and made our way back to the Ideal.

The following afternoon Roger and I drove to the Balboa Yacht Club. Suddenly I was back in America. It had been so long I had almost forgotten. The Canal Zone was home to thousands of Americans who were supporting and maintaining the Panama Canal. Roger, well received by all, did a great job of disguising himself as an American. The man from the night before arrived and soon we were off to look at a boat. I was surprised to see Roger eyeing a fourteen-foot plywood boat with a minimal outboard engine. Panama's waters have some of the greatest tidal changes in the world, making any venture on her seas a true risk. This environment mandates a strong vessel and a skilled captain and this backyard-built boat would surely not withstand the challenges. Roger counted out the cash and with a beaming smile said, "We are going fishing in the morning." Roger did not want gratitude for pulling me off the side of the road. He needed my help and, by the rules of the road, I would oblige.

I looked at the boat tied to the dock and knew I was in trouble. The boat seemed even smaller and sat too low in the water for any sizable seas. Part of me wished to walk away, part of me wanted to see what this character called a "fishing trip." My concerns doubled when Roger arrived with the supplies. The four gallons of rum sitting on top signaled that this was not a day trip. His fishing poles looked as if they had never been used, and they were not designed for ocean fishing. A large metal box and an automobile jack completed the scene.

The day was spot on perfect, not even the slightest ripple on the ocean, as we passed the breakwater. The little boat was running smoothly when Roger turned on the salsa music and mixed a drink. I sensed that he was in his element and had good fortune on his side. He steered a constant course, and the fishing poles never touched water. We never saw another boat, and five hours later some islands emerged on the horizon.

The waters turned velvet blue as we anchored in the little bay. The islands were heavily forested, and I could hear the birds squawking over the sound of the engine. Roger signaled for me to cast the fishing poles even though they lacked bait or lure. Soon we spotted two wooden canoes furiously rowing our way. Even in the distance I could sense the natives' displeasure. With their hand-carved bows and arrows drawn, they surrounded us and started screaming in a strange indigenous dialect. We both stayed cool and just sat there. Their bows tightened as Roger stood up and slowly handed the leader a gallon of rum.

After thirty seconds of silence, the leader relaxed and began to smile. All of us soon started to laugh. Five of our new friends boarded the boat and started massaging all of our belongings while jabbering constantly. They were particularly bewildered by the metal box and automobile jack. They spoke about as much Spanish as we did. When they had completed their investigation of our boat, they invited us to their village.

Open-walled thatched huts filled the perimeter of the small

clearing in the forest. Children peeked and smiled from behind their mothers' legs. The aroma of marijuana filled the air. We were invited to sit with the men in the center of the village. As if on cue, Roger turned on the music and mixed a drink. Soon the tension disappeared, and Roger and I felt at home. The children sat on my lap, despite the protest of their mothers, as we all began to drink rum and listen to Machito. Unlike the energy, the conversation was limited. The women avoided us, but the men embraced us as we went well into the night.

Waking up in the dirt is never pleasant and this morning was no exception. Groups of children surrounded me, watching for my eyes to open, while chickens pecked at my feet. I was caked with dirt and immediately went to the shore to swim in the bay. Soon most of the villagers joined me, and I could not refuse the invitation for a paddle around the island. It had been some time since I connected with the sea, and these remote people were in touch with every movement of the water. Their primitive canoes effortlessly negotiated seas that would swallow the boat I had arrived on. Walking back to the village, I was thinking these people have more than most of us.

When I returned to the village, I found Roger and a few of the village men deep in conversation. My arrival went unacknowledged. The conversation seemed to be about weights and money. From what I could discern, they were moments away from closing a deal. Everybody was pleased. Then several of the men grabbed machetes and blankets and disappeared into the jungle. The women spread woven palm mats over the ground, and Roger assembled his press from the metal box and the jack. Everybody had a job in the upcoming project, and I could sense an excitement in their pace. A massive pile of reddish weed reflected the fire's light. Dozens of villagers began chanting "fabrica, fabrica" in perfect sync with the drums. The harvest was in full swing. All cultures find hope in the harvest, and these villagers were no different. The setting was surreal, like nothing I had ever witnessed or imagined.

Eventually even the women came to trust us. In the morning we said goodbye as family. As I pulled the anchor, I could see Roger was suffering from the excess of rum and cokes. I steered us to the southeast and wondered how it was we came to gain the trust of these people so quickly. Only desperate men would have arrived in such a fashion. Our boat was small, and in their world courage was everything.

Winds came out of nowhere. An hour out from the island and four hours from the city lights the rain poured down in sheets impenetrable by the eye. The seas rose to the point that we would lose the horizon and the compass spun in the chaos. With no sense of direction, we were forced to put the bow into the waves. The only thing in our favor was a strong northwest wind; if we could keep it to our back, we should hit the mainland eventually.

The boat creaked under the pressure of the storm. All our belongings slammed freely from front to back with ankle breaking force. I spent a full hour bailing water never once lowering the ten inches of water we were standing in. Roger was surprisingly cool for a man who had little experience at sea. An hour later the storm passed and we were drifting in a calm. In every direction the sky was oblique and black as the sea and I could not tell the difference between the two. The compass had cracked and drained all fluids so that we could not tell up from down, much less east or west.

I turned on a small AM radio to see if I could pick up Panama City. Immediately I noticed that I would get a much stronger signal if I pointed the antenna to our left. In Costa Rica we had navigated our flights to and from local radio stations with an instrument that always pointed to the transmitter. My plan was to follow the strongest signal to Panama City. For the next three hours I sat on the bow with the radio glued to my ear giving Roger headings. We were running blind and getting low on fuel.

Soon I heard a strong signal coming from all directions, forcing me to abandon my plan. We had to be close. We shut down the little engine and switched to our last tank of fuel. Corking on the water in stark silence, we heard the rumble of a ship in the distance. We never did sight this ship, but we chased its wake for an hour until the lights of Panama City illuminated the horizon.

The security guard stared at us in disbelief as we tied up at the dock. We said nothing and unloaded nothing. I stepped off of the boat, too rattled to think, and Roger followed behind. Soon we were at the Ancon. Our emotions high, we spent the bulk of the night offloading the terror. Stumbling out of the door, I looked back to see Roger slumped over at the bar.

As I closed my eyes that night, all I could hear was Forbes saying, "Never know, man, might be your father."

BALANCE

The morning came and I needed to get out of Panama. As I stood at the counter of the Ideal seeking Victor's thoughts on my exodus, a well-dressed Asian man, over-hearing our conversation, approached and introduced himself as Mr. Yee. He spoke fluent English. Since I had not met anyone wearing a coat and tie in a year, I was immediately intimidated. Perceiving Mr. Yee to be an important man, I was amused when he asked me about my professional "credentials." He handed me a card and asked me to come by his office that afternoon.

Mr. Yee's office was more than an hour's walk away. As I trudged through Panama's stifling heat, I found myself wondering what new possibilities lay before me. While I was older and more battered since that wintry day my brother and I took off in the Rambler, I had not yet lost my curiosity.

Mr. Yee's office overlooked the canal, which was filled with gigantic ships. Mr. Lee acknowledged me immediately and asked me to be seated. After inquiring about my work experience, he looked at me directly.

"What has brought you to Panama?" he asked.

I hesitated a moment, debating whether or not to elaborate on my past adventures.

"I want to experience the world," I replied.

Mr. Yee scribbled something in Chinese on a small piece of paper. He handed the note to his assistant and asked him to walk me to the dock. The dock hummed with machinery. Cargo was moving in all directions, and the enormous ships made me feel miniscule. The entirely man-made clamor caused me to long for the jungle. We met a short gray-haired man at the ship and my liaison exchanged words in a language I knew I would never come to understand. Mr. Yee's assistant then shook my hand and gave me the "goodbye and good luck" glance.

The moment I boarded the Aberdeen I was in international waters and no longer in Panama. It was rare to exit a country without having my passport stamped. The Aberdeen reeked of old gear oil. Petroleum-based residue collected in every corner. Seemingly miles of dank metal halls riddled with pipes and wires led into indistinguishable rooms of exact proportion and finish. All ceilings were well below my height except for the engine room. I would spend the next month perpetually ducking.

I hired on as a mechanic's assistant, which meant I spent twelve hours a day in a 130- degree room reading gages and oiling bushings, all the while breathing diesel bypass smoke. This sweatbox was so loud from the engine noise that no one attempted to speak. I quickly learned the sign language necessary to perform my duties. Even if we could have spoken, our languages were so different that conversation would have been futile. This communication barrier made all social gatherings and meals awkward at first. Moreover, I was the only westerner on the boat and these men were real sailors. I had heard that sailors go to sea to avoid civilization. Many of them are lost on land and often choose between jail or the ocean. Truly incorrigible, they live in the confines of the ship foregoing temptation. I found these confines stifling.

My reputation as a hard worker eventually eased my entry into the group and soon I was invited to share the table for meals. I kept to myself and spent the bulk of my off time on deck, desperate for fresh air. I made several attempts to engage the captain in conversation but was readily dismissed.

After more days of smoke, noise, and boredom than I care to recall, we anchored in the Gulf of Thailand. I collected my pay and boarded a supply vessel bound for Bangkok. As we entered the Chao Praya River, I spotted several overloaded rice barges so burdened they could only travel downstream. I was enchanted by all the teak houses built on stilts emerging above beds of river hyacinth. The architecture here was dazzling. Ornate palaces with sheer roofs of gold and meticulously carved dragons at each end gleamed in the sunlight. Toward evening we chugged past towering, complex temples adorned with inlaid precious stones which reflected the city lights. I felt as if I was in another world entirely. I knew that Asia would profoundly change me.

I was ill-prepared for the sensory overload that is Bangkok. Nothing looked, sounded or smelled familiar. I was standing in the midst of constant whirling motion. Myriads of indefinable wheeled vehicles charged at me in a frenzied, constant pace. Strangers surrounded me. Everywhere everything was for sale. Over the clamor and the motorcycles I could hear the natives chattering in Thai, a language that seemed to be an octave higher than most. I could not comprehend a single word.

I was just standing there trying to regroup when Mr. Lim pulled over in what looked like a racing golf cart. He looked at me and I climbed in back. I noticed that his silk shirt and trousers badly needed laundering. We shot out to the six-lane road and barely caught the gap between a converging cement truck and a bus. Changing four lanes at a time was common, and here inches were plenty of separation from anything moving or not. Arriving at the Ambassador Hotel, I thought if I ever found life to be boring I would just take another ride with Mr. Lim. I was to learn that in Asia there is always someone waiting for you.

I had been in the bush too long. Every venture forth from the

Ambassador that night left me numb from the input. Numerous small markets spilled onto the streets offering goods from all corners of the world. Women constantly vied for my attention. I could buy anything in this city and almost all behavior was acceptable. I found this freedom an immense responsibility every time I walked out of the door.

The following morning I found a smiling Mr. Lim waiting in front of the Ambassador. Figuring that he was probably well ahead of me, I wished him “good morning” and we were off. Mr. Lim loved the chase and the adrenal charge of Bangkok’s roads. As before, he delivered an unforgettable ride. At river’s edge we boarded a very colorful long wooden boat with a twenty-foot long propeller shaft that could easily be pulled out of the water and spun in all directions. We rocketed through an intricate maze of narrow waterways, barely missing swimmers, other boats and the stilt houses built over the river.

The waterways were as congested, frenzied and chaotic as the roads. Children would jump off of their river porches as water buffalo grazed at the water’s edge. When several waterways merged, timeless ladies dressed in brightly embroidered garb and bamboo hats sold vegetables from their tiny canoes. Up close, the palaces and temples were even more impressive, housing magnificent solid golden Buddhas of all sizes. The people of Thailand unavoidably embraced their past, a powerful sense of history filling each wall in this magical corner of the world.

Mr. Lim dropped me at the train station and helped me secure a ticket to Chiang Mai. I thanked him emphatically for his service, and we parted knowing we would see each other again. Nothing at the train station was written in English, but I found my train with the help of a very cute kid. It was an overnight run to Chiang Mai, and I splurged and spent the extra two dollars for a shared sleeper cabin.

The Thai countryside lay flat with deep green rice paddies fanning out in every direction. The train stopped often and I took the opportunity to survey my surroundings. It was a relief not to be careening through city streets. I spent that day in deep reflection. The past is never far.

An ancient city, Chiang Mai was a mix of Burma, Laos and Thailand due to the proximity of each country. A large open-air market filled the town center with a display of countless foods and products, none of which I had seen before. Pedaled rickshaw, the main method of transportation, confirmed that I was indeed in Asia. Although the streets were much less congested than in Bangkok, I still had to be wary of my every move. I checked into the hotel across from the market and sat on the roof drinking beers with some Canadians. Thailand attracted travelers from all over the world, and I could often get my best information from like-minded people.

I was walking through the streets of Chiang Mai in search of dinner when Chao joined my step. He appeared to be younger than me, and he spoke understandable English. Resembling an Asian John Lennon, he immediately captured my trust. Chao told me that he led treks into the hill tribe villages north of Chiang Mai, and he was seeking clientele. Attracted by his energy, I signed up.

The next morning a small truck was waiting for me in front of the hotel. Next to the Chao sat another man of modest proportion. Chao introduced me to Rama as I climbed in the truck. Rama, who appeared to be a good friend of Chao's, spoke no English. The two chattered in their high-pitched manner as we headed north. The road ended at a small river where we purchased food from a roadside market before jumping into a hand-carved riverboat. Motoring up river, we passed tiny villages and bamboo groves so tall they covered the river from one side to the other. Elephants played with the children at the water's edge. All is well with the world, I thought.

When the river became too shallow, we stepped off and walked north for a few hours until we arrived at a Karen village. The Karen, like most Hill Tribes in this lawless and border-free part of Asia, lived in huts built of bamboo elevated off of the ground. Their handmade clothes were adorned with multicolored embroidery, and copious amounts of earrings hung down to their shoulders. The children played, the women worked, and the men lay around in huts smoking opium. In fact it was rare even to see a man, and the village women took great pride in harassing them for their non-performance. On our journey we had passed large fields of opium poppies. I gathered that smoking opium did not lead to a productive life.

The village chickens ran from me and the pigs followed me everywhere, hoping I needed to go to the bathroom. The Karen slept on hard bamboo floors built above the ground to avoid the rains and snakes. For me a good night's rest was virtually impossible.

With the morning sun came elephants crashing through the trees. These were working pachyderms used to harvest hardwoods. However, for the next few days they were to be our transportation. People of this part of the world establish lifetime relationships with their elephants and treat them as family. I boarded my elephant using the ramp at the end of the deck. Once aboard, I wrapped my legs around the elephant's head and quickly learned to move in sync with her. Her skin was rough with stiff prickly hairs that penetrated my clothing. Impossibly sure-footed, this gentle giant could traverse very steep terrain without once forcing me to grab hold.

I soon learned not to look down when we crossed streams, as invariably the elephants would suck up five gallons of water to spray their bodies. Even the slightest peek over the side would deliver a bucketful of mucus-filled spray directly to my face. For no particular reason, I called my elephant "Daisy." We would stop during the day and wash the elephants in the river in sincere appreciation for their assistance and kindness. This was a special time. It brought out the child in all of us.

This jungle was not as thick as Panama's and relatively devoid of wildlife. We climbed all afternoon and when we arrived at an Akah Village, set on top of the ridge, the flames were just about to reach the huts. Chao looked startled, Rama remained calm, and the elephants were passive. The villagers were frantically collecting their paltry possessions, placing them in the village center in hopes of saving them from the rapidly encroaching fire. Chao, Rama and I joined in with the villagers and began fighting the fire with buckets of water and dirt, all the while drowning in a sea of soot, ash and smoke. An hour or so later, the winds shifted and blew the fire down the mountainside. We looked around and realized in an instant that we had almost lost it all.

The villagers now accepted us as family and soon we were summoned to the chief's hut. Swimming in seas of sisal, the hut was lit with candles equally spaced apart on the floor. Dressed like the Karen, Akah women attended each light. The chief humbly thanked us for our help and invited us to lie on the floor next to each candle. The aroma of burning rubber filled the room.

Soon the conversation in the hut became loud and persistent. I could see Chao was uncomfortable as we sat with the chief discussing the origin of the fire. I learned that the Thai government had recently subsidized the village for planting crops other than opium to the immense displeasure of Kusar, a Burmese drug lord. Kusar was wreaking havoc in the region, and most of the villages had resumed growing poppies to avoid his wrath. The chief was deeply contemplating his decision. An elderly man of shrunken physical stature, the chief was constantly lost in thought. I could see in his eyes that Kusar had won, and I suspected the chief was willing to accept this fact. The Hill Tribes of this region had nowhere else to go.

We continued north into Burma, following narrow trails overgrown with flowering vines. We navigated by the sun, and everyone enjoyed the leisurely pace of an elephant's life. We would cherish river crossings, each time taking the opportunity to swim. Just before sunset, we crossed the ridge of a high mountain and I could see a village in the valley below. I was lagging behind when I heard gunshots and Daisy bolted into the brush. Jungle branches peeled me off of her back and I crashed down onto the jungle floor, landing on my left arm. The pain was excruciating, but I knew I could not scream. I could hear men in the distance yelling in a language I had not yet heard as I bit my tongue in agony.

Lying silent in the jungle, I faded in and out of consciousness. It had to be Kusar. I awoke to Daisy nudging my chest with her trunk. Her eyes were as wide as mine. She knew I was in trouble. I grabbed hold of her trunk, and she helped me to my feet. It was pitch dark as we set out for the village. I could not hoist myself onto Daisy's back, so we walked side by side down the mountain. Sensing my pain, Daisy would comfort me with the occasional gentle touch to my head with her trunk as we headed for the village in the valley.

This village had no lights, but I could hear Chao talking rapidly in Thai. The absence of women and children meant trouble. I was in need of help and knew that somehow I must contend. A dozen or so men wearing army fatigues were standing around the fire interrogating Chao. There was no sign of Rama. I made sure they could hear me arrive, and soon I was met with rifles pointed in my direction.

I fell to the ground clutching my arm. At a glance these soldiers appeared to be young kids, but I had learned that judging age in Asia was impossible. With no apparent leader, the men circled me and began to shout in what I had to assume was Burmese. I longed for a gray-haired man with whom I could reason. I said nothing and decided to fall unconscious.

Out of the dark, the women collected me and I was rushed into a hut. They fashioned a splint out of bamboo and poured local whiskey down my throat. The children sat with me and began rubbing my feet. I needed their help, and they knew it.

Chao woke me at dawn.

"We have to leave now," he whispered with urgency.

I struggled to my feet, noticing that that the village seemed to have been abandoned overnight. We headed south toward the river while I tried to clear the cobwebs from my brain. The splint was heavy and awkward. Chao never spoke of the previous night and I never asked. A few hours later we arrived at a wide river flowing gently east. Chao began chopping bamboo while I peeled the skin for lashing ropes. Just before sundown our raft was completed, and we glided down river. The raft floated effortlessly, and we used long bamboo poles to push away from the banks. Navigating any river at night was an immense risk, but I could sense that Chao was running.

Around midnight we arrived at a small village set on the riverbank. We were well received by the local people whom Chao seemed to know. Feasting on banana pancakes and whiskey, we finally relaxed. I was treated well but regarded only as an observer. Nobody questioned my circumstance or asked about my past, leading me to conclude that everybody remains anonymous in lands without laws or borders.

We set out the next morning. The river narrowed and we had to shoot a few small rapids which never failed to relieve the tension. Thick jungle trees and vines intertwined along the river, and we would be delighted when we came upon groups of wild elephants and small troops of monkeys. As the river widened, we spotted villages along the banks. Arriving in Chiang Rai we were swarmed by dozens of children splashing in the water, each with a pet snake. As soon as they sensed my fear of snakes, they took great joy in pushing them in my face for my inevitable reaction.

This was an outpost town of simple architecture and everyone looked at me as if I was trouble. I went in search of a doctor while Chao disappeared into the streets. There were no hotels in town, but I was able to rent a guesthouse behind the market. No one spoke English. It took me most of the afternoon to locate a doctor. His office, unswept for a decade, contained several countertops all filled with bottles of herbs and potions. The language barrier proved challenging, but he ultimately got his point across by pointing at my arm and snapping a pencil in half. With that he graciously opened the door and bowed. I spent the next two days resting in the guesthouse, clutching my crude bamboo splint, tiring of sleeping on one side.

Chao arrived early in the morning and announced that we were off to the Golden Triangle. We jumped in the back of a dilapidated truck and sat down next to the smiling Rama. I wanted to ask Rama where he had gone but thought better of it. The day was lovely and my arm began to feel better. We passed two roadblocks without issue, which both surprised and puzzled me.

Standing on the edge of the Mekong River, I could see Burma and Laos simultaneously. We dislodged a large bamboo raft that was tied to a tree and set sail. The Mekong was coffee-brown from sediment as we crossed into Laos. This majestic river has history for Americans, and I was concerned about how well I would be received. Chao and Rama seemed relaxed, so I followed with the same energy. Many parts of the river were too deep for our poles to steer, so we were often at the mercy of the current. There was very little traffic on this river. At midday we caught a low hanging tree branch and tied up in front of a small village.

We were well received by the Laotians. Unlike the hill tribes, the men did all of the interacting with us. Chao spoke the language and had a knack for putting everyone at ease quickly. We were invited for lunch and the villagers soon gathered to see the strangers. Sitting in the dirt in the village center, surrounded by huts overgrown with jungle vines, we all ate rice and river fish. The children would sneak up from behind to touch me. I was truly an anomaly but apparently not considered a threat.

An elderly man grabbed my arm and gestured for me to follow him into the forest. As a guest, I could not refuse. At the end of the trail we came upon a small river tributary and a hand-carved riverboat. I could see that the engine had been taken apart and I jumped in to have a look. We spent the rest of the afternoon assembling the engine while the children watched with fascination. A few hours later the engine coughed to life, and the old man smiled for the first time that day.

We left an hour before sunset. The villagers thanked us with a bucket full of rice and vegetables and forty feet of heavy fishing line. We floated all night in total darkness and pouring rain. Often we would get so cold that we would jump into the river and hang onto the raft wondering what creatures lay below. At sunrise we stopped at a beach and got some sleep lying in the sun. We spent the afternoon collecting shrimp under rocks in the shallow water and once again set off down river.

I could see that Chao and Rama were not fisherman, but soon our line was in the water and tied to the raft. We would pass the occasional village, observing the bewilderment of the locals at the sight of our raft. Suddenly the raft lunged sideways and I spilled into the water. I thought we had hit a rock, but I could tell from the screams of Rama that we had caught a fish. The raft was bouncing in all directions and I was drifting too fast to get back on. Rama and Chao clung to the sides of the raft, making no effort to pull in the fish. I swam to the bank. As the raft passed me, I could see what appeared to be a fish as large as the raft itself violently thrashing on the surface of the water.

"Cut him loose!" I yelled.

But they just kept hanging on in shock. I jumped back in the river and swam to the raft, carefully avoiding the massive fish. Most of our belongings had been tossed into the river, and I could not find the machete. When the fish finally dragged us close to the riverbank, we all jumped in and held onto the raft which proved to be an equal match in strength. Rama and Chao were screaming what I assumed to be expletives in Thai. Eventually we saw the humor in our plight and began to laugh.

At that very moment I saw the first crocodile coming across the river. Rama also spotted him and we quickly climbed onto the raft, yanking Chao aboard. The fish turned the raft around, and we all grabbed our poles. All at once the crocodiles attacked the fish, ripping huge hunks out of his side, spinning to peel the flesh from the bones. At the height of this primal frenzy dozens of crocodiles devoured the enormous fish tethered to our raft. The feeding went on for more than an hour as we watched in fascination and fear. We spent most of that afternoon swatting the crocodiles with our bamboo poles until they were sated and finally returned to the shore.

Around the bend we came upon another village and stopped to rest. Chao began relating our story of the fish and crocodiles to an enthralled crowd. The people on the river again were willing to take us in, even though we were an odd three. If I had arrived at any of these villages on my own, I would have been met with more suspicion and concern. Traveling with Chao and Rama removed that dynamic. This worked both ways. My presence would equally relieve the concerns of all, making us seem harmless. I suspect that Chao knew this well.

The Mekong transitioned into a large gorge bordered by sheer limestone cliffs of stark beauty. The only action here was the occasional overpowered brightly painted boat screaming by at extraordinary speed. Surely these boats were designed to outrun the law. But from what I could ascertain, there was no law on the Mekong. Chao always took keen notice of these boats. Since Chao had preferred not to stop at larger towns on the river, I was surprised to find him willing to stop in Luang Prabang.

There were more than a hundred carved riverboats lined up at the river's edge. Tying up next to them, we stepped from boat to boat to get ashore. A large city, Luang Prabang was not as chaotic as Bangkok. There was a relative serenity in this exotic place. The palaces were as extraordinary as Bangkok's, and I could visit them as if they were mine. The townspeople were considerate and seemed to enjoy my presence. I found a hotel with a pool since I desperately needed the chlorine to heal my many bug bites from the river.

As usual, Chao and Rama disappeared. After soaking an hour in the pool, I explored the back streets and wandered among the many open markets. The collection of bizarre river foods astounded me. Blanched toads, river slugs and fish heads the size of a turkey were prominently displayed as the Laotian women constantly fanned away the flies. Markets were the source of life and provided perhaps the only occasion during which all walks of life interacted. Since refrigeration was rare, most people traveled the river daily to purchase or trade for food. The markets provided a glimpse into the life of the region and never failed to be entertaining. I was enjoying my time in Luang Prabang and was troubled to see the look in Chao's eyes when he returned. He did not have to say a word. I collected my things and climbed back across the boats to reach our raft.

The jungle soon gave way to miles of lowlands planted in a variety of crops, mostly rice. The river traffic increased with wooden barges laden with crops and hard working people. These barges often traveled at the same speed and occasionally we would tie up and share stories. We spent nights sleeping on the riverbank, and I noticed that Chao stopped looking over his shoulder. Conversation among us became infrequent and rambling. I could sense my companions were weary and missed their homes. Indeed I could empathize. I did not know where this journey would end, but I knew it was not my call.

EXILE

Just outside of Vientiane we tied up the raft and walked toward the highway. Without explanation, Chao walked back and untied the raft. I chose not to comment, feeling I was saying goodbye to an old friend. We waved down a truck and jumped in back on a load of green beans. Vientiane had little of the charm of Luang Prabang and looked more like a business center. I could see Chao looking across the river into Thailand, lost in reflection. Chao was certainly more complex than I had originally read. He yelled at the driver in Thai, and we turned east away from the river.

When the truck stopped in front of a palatial residence, I presumed we had run out of gas. Chao jumped down and paid the driver. I followed while Rama stayed in the truck. We banged the gong in front of the intricately carved teak gate and were greeted by a Thai gentlemen spotlessly dressed in a white coat and white gloves. He summoned us in and led us through a maze of exquisite gardens with ornate sculpture and lotus ponds.

At the house we were passed off to four of the loveliest woman I had ever seen who took us to our respective rooms. They drew my bath and set out some clean clothes. Sinking into the marble tub, I was totally out of my element. Smelling of lavender soap, I sat on the edge of the bed completely baffled as to what I was to do next.

A beautiful woman knocked on the door and led me to a round table in the elaborately flowered courtyard. Chao was engaged in an intense conversation with a large Asian man who was drinking scotch. My arrival did not phase them. I knew this was a conversation that could only take place between a father and son. I sat, sipping tea, hoping they would offer me a scotch. It did not take Chao long to lighten the exchange, and I took the opportunity to introduce myself.

Chao's father spoke flawless English with authority and, like his son, put me at immediate ease. Following a crafty five-minute interrogation, he welcomed me to his home and poured me a drink. He longed for conversation which signaled that he was exiled in his own palace. The finest meal I had eaten in a year was served, and we spoke late into the night about the differences between east and west. I barely recall going to bed that night, but before falling asleep I made sure to clear the room of crocodiles.

Waking in disbelief at my surroundings, I explored the gardens and swam in the pool. My breakfast was delivered along with the Bangkok Post. I had not read a newspaper in months, and found it hard to connect with the world's plight. I was still digesting the recent week's events, pondering fate or destiny, when Chao interrupted my musings by tapping on my shoulder.

"Let's go," he said.

Out front Rama was leaning against a new Mercedes. Well south of town we boarded a large ferryboat filled with Laotians, pigs, chickens and bags of rice. The captain was obviously troubled by my presence, and Chao went to work settling the issue. Chao confided that I might not be well received in Cambodia. He had to promise the captain that I would stay out of sight. From the look on the captain's face, I suspected he had been hoodwinked into allowing me aboard.

This aging ferry, leaking from several critical points, was under constant bail from the captain's many children. A sisal canopy covered the bulk of the hull, amplifying the painfully loud engine noise and ensuring that most of the exhaust gas remained inside. Despite the ferry's ungainly appearance, the ancient riverboat moved swiftly down the Mekong.

There were perhaps thirty of us on board. Since there were no seats, we sat on large bags of rice. The captain insisted I wear a traditional bamboo hat and soon the soot from the engine blackened my skin. I was to run the river anonymously, a position I had grown accustomed to. The captain's children took to me immediately, but the captain never did. He was a tall, painfully thin man whose eyes reflected a dark past.

In particular I was drawn to a four-year old girl named Taqi. We would play for hours inventing games with fruit. Taqi knew nothing but kindness and possessed timeless beauty. She filled my days with optimism as only a child could. She had a bad cough that seemed to worry no one but me.

We would stop at random villages for fuel and I was told to stay out of sight. Peeking through holes in the sisal, I would see men dressed in military clothing, many with only one leg. In this stretch of the Mekong everything was scrutinized and it was difficult to know who was in authority. The Thai side of the river was more productive with people at work wherever the land allowed. On the Laotian side the land was either unworked or left fallow.

I relished the nights as I could climb up top and get some fresh air while catching glimpses of life on the river. The night brought peace to this turbulent section of the river. We crossed into Cambodia about two in the morning, and I could see the captain tense up. There was no formal checkpoint, but the mood on the boat darkened. I trusted the perceptions were real and hurriedly went below.

At daybreak I heard the captain screaming while two boats approached on each side. Several men, armed with large rifles, instantly boarded our boat. The children huddled around me. Taqi began to cry and jumped in my arms. Chao spoke before the captain had uttered a word, taking control of the situation. Four armed men came below and dragged me to the bow. Chao, as usual, was working on the leader and paid no attention to my arrival. I stood there in submission, looking at my feet. The conversation was crisp and, for the first time, I heard Chao raise his voice in defiance. I assumed this to be a risky, last ditch effort. The leader smiled and Chao did not return it. I could see this river game was at a stalemate, noticing that the captain was shaking. Then the armed men departed as quickly as they arrived. We all knew we had been very lucky.

We tied up at a small tributary and spent the day swimming in the shade. Taqi loved to swim and she spent the afternoon jumping off of the bow, giggling with delight. At sundown we made our way back to the river and motored all night, reminding me of Salvador. The captain shut off the engine at first sight of the lights of Phnom Penh. It was after midnight, and we could not judge distance from the lights' reflection on the river. The current was gentle as we tied up on a dark vacant dock.

Once off the boat, Chao stopped a van and we quickly crawled in back. Arriving at a modest hotel, we were hurriedly escorted to a basement room. A few minutes later Chao left, again without uttering a single word. I was on edge and despite having the first bed I had seen in many days, I could not sleep. To the dislike of the gentleman behind the hotel desk, I went out onto the streets in the morning. There were more motorcycles than people, making it nearly impossible to cross the street. I learned to cross one lane at a time, holding my ground as countless motorcycles brushed by. Nobody stood still and no one ever approached me. In every muddy alley a freelance market could be found. Farmers and craftsman would travel for days to sell their wares in any open spot. The currency here was thin and tattered, confirming that this was a struggling country.

Long before I saw it, I could smell the huge central market. Multi-colored tarps shaded a maze of muddy trails filled with a millennium's discard. Dismembered animal parts drew flies like waste. Bucket after bucket of indefinable insects and invertebrates were spoiling as I passed by. Everything dripped. The negotiations between vendor and customer were rabid. Every sense I possessed was engaged. I found a quiet corner to collect my emotions when I was approached by a thin man with one eye. Glancing in all directions, he offered me the opportunity to blow up a water buffalo with a rocket launcher. I just stood there, thinking none of this could be happening.

Walking back to the hotel, I knew I needed to get out of this town. In front of the hotel Chao was waiting in a car. He looked scared as he reached over to open the door. We were on the same page. We knew we had to get back to Thailand. We had entered Cambodia illegally so we would have to enter Thailand the same. When we arrived at the ferry, I received my first smile from the captain as he threw me my hat. Taqi was asleep, so I just kissed her gently on her head. By the sun I could see we were heading north. After a month of southbound travel, I knew this direction would bring change. The river was auspiciously quiet and fear caught in my throat.

Although paranoia was new to me, I had to accept it as the price of the journey. We were running by day again. It was all or nothing. Chao explained that we were hoping to join a refugee route leading to Thailand. The Khmer had recently lost Phnom Penh to the Vietnamese, and many Cambodians were fleeing to Thailand. Motoring up river proved to be excruciatingly slow and the sighting of any boat or village would stop our breath.

Taqi kept chasing the chickens around the boat, oblivious to the danger. I longed to be innocent again. There was no point to my staying below anymore. We would no longer be seen as a hapless river ferry. With the night came calm. Nobody slept but the children. The river opened into a gigantic lake and we chose to cross the center. It was refreshing to be able to see in all directions, no longer wondering what was lurking in the jungle. Many people, perpetually drifting in shanty floating villages, made this lake their home. Their small barges housed as many as ten people and all of life's essentials were strapped to every available post. Pigs in tiny floating pens were lashed to the back, and chickens scratched and pecked on the roof. A constant fire burned on the back of every home. Nobody looked at us and nobody waved.

The setting sun showcased the pillars of Angkor Wat towering above the rainforest. I had seen pictures of Angkor as a child, but they did little justice to the magnificence of this setting. We tied up to a tree next to the impenetrable jungle. Taqi came to say goodbye and we both cried. The captain, totally out of character, gave me a hug while retrieving his hat from my head.

"Good luck," he muttered in English.

"Please take care of my little girl," I replied, holding his gaze. He smiled and nodded in understanding.

Catching the last glimpse of my boat friends in the darkness, I knew they would make it through any interrogation. Fugitives do not travel with children.

Hacking through the forest, I finally understood why no one named a boat on the Mekong. In this part of the world, people traveled anonymously. We came upon a small stream and followed up current. Our progress was tedious, and we slept in a small clearing. It felt good to walk, reminding me of Corcovado and the long slog through that jungle. We saw smoke in the distance and decided to investigate. We were crossing a fallow field when a voice yelled from the forest. Chao froze.

"We are in a minefield," he said in a shaky voice.

All of the hundreds of one-legged people I had seen in Cambodia rushed through my mind. I could see Chao was no longer in control.

"Follow me," I said in a steady voice.

We had left footprints in the young grass and carefully retraced our every step. Chao lapsed into silence. I tapped his shoulder, and he followed me as we circled the field until we came upon a trail and continued north.

When I saw the group of men, I decided not to miss a step, noting they were traveling with food and not weapons. They looked at me as if I had come from outer space, speaking quickly among themselves. I smiled and sat down next to them. A minute later the awkward silence broke as we all laughed. Chao remained silent. Walking with them that afternoon, I suspected my new friends were considering all of the potentials of my presence. We sat in the jungle that night drinking homemade whiskey, communicating by drawing in the dirt with sticks. Our common struggle drew us closer. Dressed in worn military clothing and of similar bone structure, it was impossible for me to tell them apart. These men were Khmer and I was banking on the hope that they were on the run and not on the job. Regardless, this was their country and I needed their help to get out.

The next day went smoothly and when we arrived at a river of significant size, I knew it would lead to Thailand. Chao was pulling out of his near catatonic state. I was swimming off the dust when I noticed that our friends from the night before had disappeared. Before I could turn around, I heard the boat coming up the river. They were on me before I could swim to the shore. Plucked from the water, I lay on the floor, staring up at their well-polished gun barrels. I looked over to see Chao surrounded on the shore. This was the real thing.

The Khmer were machine-like and went about their business

meticulously. Life was incidental in their world, and this was evident in their eyes. We were loaded into a jeep, which had a rocket launcher strapped to the roll bars, and driven into the forest. The simple mounting of the rocket launcher showed they were as desperate as me. I took comfort in this, knowing they were not here by choice either. The camp was cleverly hidden under shade trees with minimal debris. They had not been there long. They tossed me into a pit eight feet deep and covered the top with palm fronds. From the strong smell of human waste, I knew I was not the first one to anoint this pit. Standing in total darkness, I wondered how long I would last before I had to sit in the quagmire, all the while thinking how brilliant their tactics were. In the darkness time was lost. I could have been there for hours or days.

I would hear the occasional rumble of an engine or the barking of a command. I assumed these men were nomadic and hiding for a reason. Certainly they would not waste much time on my fate. The sound of a hovering helicopter broke the delirium. The Khmer were screaming and running, and I could hear the jeeps' engines fire up. Then there was silence. I had to risk looking, so I carved steps in the dirt with a rock. Peeking through the palms, I saw nothing. As I climbed out of the pit, my heart was beating out of my chest. No one was in sight, not even Chao. I ran to the forest and turned back to look for him. The camp was small, and there was only one pit. I knew I had to move quickly. Running through the forest, I kept thinking to myself, "Where is Chao?"

A few miles later I pushed my way into the deep forest to rest. I was exhausted and dehydrated. I spent the day eating jungle fruit and hiding in the brush. I followed a tiny stream until I found the river and continued north. When the occasional boat motored down river, I would throw myself to the ground. Any sign of human life would send me back to the forest where movement was painfully slow. The nights were long and restless.

The next morning I decided to climb a small mountain to get an overview of the area. In the distance I could see miles of rice fields. I thought that had to be Thailand. I walked the dirt levies that divided the rice fields and came upon some railroad tracks. Following the tracks well into the night, I finally sighted a station in the distance. Many people were loitering about and from the roadside camps I could see they had been waiting for days.

I was relieved when few took notice of my arrival. Working myself into the crowd I sat down, hoping to be inconspicuous. Most of the people were speaking Thai, but I had no idea what country I was in and I could not dare to ask. The crowd was unsavory and many could use a bath. Most had very little in the way of personal possessions, and I sensed that the train would not arrive soon. I fit in perfectly with this crowd.

Hearing the train in the distance, the crowd began to stir. Feverishly they stuffed their belongings into plastic bags and set about gathering their children. As the small train screeched to a halt, I could see this would be a competitive process as there were more passengers than seats. Asians were masters of cutting you off in lines, so I knew my best play would be the roof. Stuffed shoulder to shoulder, we pulled out of the station in the heat of the midday sun.

As we slowly passed by miles and miles of rice paddies, I was glad to see the train was on a westerly course. The hats of the people working the rice fields confirmed that I was back in Thailand. The heat was intense, especially when we would stop at rural stations while another hundred people attempted to squeeze into the impossibly overloaded train. I did not have the strength to even ponder my time in Cambodia and the lessons therein. However, I knew from that point forward in my life I would strive to be successful, never wishing to be a refugee again.

The sky grayed from the smoke of Bangkok as the train slowed outside of the city. I followed the lead of the others and jumped off. Trudging the last few miles, I was truly lost. For the first time in my life, I was not sure which way to go. I had left a small bag with clothes and some money at the Ambassador and dearly hoped it was still under their care. The security guard at the Ambassador was reluctant to even let me in the door. This was the sure sign I had hit bottom.

In the midst of the ruckus, the manager came over and I explained I was a past guest at his fine establishment and had stored my valuables while I was away. He viewed me suspiciously but returned a few minutes later with my bag. I got a room and took the longest shower of my life. I mostly slept for the next twenty-four hours, wandering out only for food.

The Khmer had taken my passport, and I was almost out of money. It was time to leave Asia. Mr. Lim was overjoyed to see me and shook my hand vigorously as I greeted him in front of the Ambassador. Sitting in his Tuk Tuk, he turned around and looked at me.

"To the port, sir," he said. No reply was necessary. He could read it in my eyes.

Ricocheting through Bangkok's traffic seemed normal now. Mr. Lim was, as usual, on top of his game. Stuffed into the seat pocket in front of me was a copy of the Bangkok Post. On the front cover was a picture of Chao in a military officer's uniform. The title read "High Ranking Government Official Freed from Khmer in Jungle Raid." The article went on to describe the heroics of the raid and the continuing search for the missing American. I was staring in disbelief when we arrived at the port. Mr. Lim spun around with a big smile.

"No charge, sir, and I will let the embassy know you are well."

TIMELESS

Without a passport, I could only depart Thailand as a sailor. Fortunately, I had received a good review from my last sailing on the Aberdeen. The Victoria was a supply ship based out of Australia, and I suspected I was selected by race. The Australians I had met were fun-loving people and I was ready for some western exposure. The ship was predictably dank, but the energy of the crew sparkled. When not on duty, they played loud rock and roll music and drank constantly. Their irreverent wit appealed to me, and I often laughed until I cried. Such desperate gaiety had to have come from genuine struggle.

There was little hierarchy on the Victoria. It was common the see the captain drinking with the cook. Docking in Kota Kinabalu, I was shocked to see a very large city. I had always pictured Borneo as the end of the road. Predominantly monochrome industrial buildings filled the skylines, and the blanket of smoke and soot made breathing a challenge.

Every port had a bar just outside the loading docks, and this is where I found the captain sitting next to large European man wearing a tee shirt. I had come to know the captain well, having spent many nights drinking bitters while listening to the Rolling Stones. He introduced me to Ron who poured me a scotch from the open bottle on the table. An affable guy, Ron radiated optimism from every pore. From the feel of his handshake, I could tell he worked hard and often. An underwater welder, he had done work on the Victoria last time she was in port. We shared diving stories over dinner and opened another bottle of scotch.

Desiring to change his line of work, Ron had been exploring Eastern Borneo for a place to build a dive resort. He had discovered a seamount in remote Eastern Borneo with spectacular diving and was in town seeking investors. Successful in that pursuit, he was spending his days filling a truck with supplies for his new endeavor. The captain immediately knew why I had knocked on his door. He explained that they would be back in Kota Kinabalu in sixty days and that I was welcome back on board at any time.

In the morning I found Ron eating breakfast, sweating out the evening's scotch in the sun.

"You drive," he said, pointing toward a small truck.

As I anticipated, Kota Kinabalu's streets were hopelessly congested. It was the law of the jungle again, and I was totally rusty. But once outside of Kota Kinabalu, Borneo opened up into a glorious maze of mountains and valleys of dense tropical rainforest. I had come to know most tropical plants, yet did not recognize a single tree or plant here. Almost every bend in the highway brought another unnamed river lined with beautiful flowering trees. Everything seemed especially large to me and I sensed that this was actually what the earth looked like sixty thousand years ago.

Considering the never-ending line of rusted logging trucks heading west, the highway was in good condition. All the flatlands were planted with endless rows of oil palms. Ron spent the time sketching designs on scratch paper. Later that afternoon we arrived in the coastal city of Sandakan. The heat was stifling. Ron dropped me at the market and gave me directions to a bar where I was to meet him later.

Despite the heat of the day, the market, a four-story concrete open-air building, was filled with shoppers and tradesmen. All manner of tidal sea creatures flopped around in buckets. This market was quite different from the markets on the Mekong. Sea slugs the size of a loaf of bread were surrounded by pails dripping with slimy mollusks. I saw thirty or forty varieties of tiny crabs, most dead for several days. You could smell this market from ten miles away. Spiked fruit the size of a watermelon hung from trees, reeking of rotting flesh but tasting of honey. By far the oddest delicacies were raw turtle eggs. I would gag just watching as the locals slurped the large shells dry. It was this sight that drove me back to the street.

I had become accustomed to the dangers of any sidewalk in a developing country, but this city proved to be even more perilous. At every third step I had to maneuver around gaping holes, many filled with high voltage wires. I learned to walk with my eyes cast down at my feet all the while listening carefully for motorized threats. At the water's edge I came upon a collection of small weather-damaged homes built on stilts over the ocean. Intertwined with bowed planks, I would often have to pass through one home to reach another. No one took notice of me, and no one had anything to hide. All waste went through the holes in the floors and I hoped the planks would support my weight and keep me out of the quagmire. Both children and adults, although shy, appeared unconcerned by my presence. They seemed to view me as theater.

I worked my way along the dirt roads following the sea and found Ron sitting next to a local man wearing a bright red sarong and a broad grin. Immediately I perceived that Walid was a man of small proportion but enormous substance. He carried the confidence that comes from survival, and his eyes reflected empathy.

Ron was seeking to hire men from Walid's village since they were renowned builders of sturdy structures that could meet the extreme requirements of Eastern Borneo. Ron suggested I travel with Walid and assist him in assembling the crew, an offer I eagerly accepted. Even though life had taught me never to get on a motorcycle, particularly in this part of the world, I soon found myself part of a one man race through the alleys of Sandakan.

Walid thrilled to the chase, and I could hear him laughing over the screaming engine. We zoomed through the rainforest for an hour, coming to a halt at the river's edge. The forest sang out with the shrieks of gibbons and the squawks of tropical birds. We boarded a small wooden boat and drifted downstream. While Walid tried to start the engine, I bailed the rainwater. We both could hear that the spark plug was fouled and accepted our fate with a simple shrug and continued floating down the river. Walid spoke little English, but we communicated effortlessly.

The dense jungle that smothered the riverbanks pulsed with life. Many varieties of monkeys I had never seen would scatter as we rounded the river bends. By far the oddest monkeys were the Proboscis with their massive noses that looked strikingly human. In the rare clearing, pigmy elephants chomped on jungle leafs, completely indifferent to our presence. It was like starting all over for me; I was seeing everything for the first time.

As the river widened we came upon a floating city made of hardwood logs, literally a mile-long parade of lashed logs gliding to market. More than twenty men lived on this floating city that offered most of the comforts of home. We tied up and Walid took off to clean the spark plug. The loggers welcomed me with the offer of a cold beer. At a glance, I sensed that they had been in the bush too long. This was a renegade's life and they seemed intrigued by my intrusion into their world. Walid returned with the spark plug, and the engine came to life just as the rains set in.

We continued down river for several hours. Turning into a small tributary, we tied up at a thoroughly battered dock. Walid poured what appeared to be a mix of oil and gasoline over his legs and arms. He offered this vile mixture to me but I declined.

The trail was narrow and the scale of the plants and trees left me feeling two feet tall. Every leaf in the forest was large enough to provide us shelter from the rain.

It was not long before I regretted my decision not to smear my body with the foul smelling petroleum. Up to now I had observed that few animals live up to their reputations. The leech, however, delivered as promised. I never even felt these four-inch fanged slugs latch on to my skin, nor was I aware of the copious amounts of blood they extracted from me. At first sighting every instinct I possessed demanded that I rip them off instantly. However, this unintelligent act would reward me with a fountain of my own blood spurting with such force that it would take several minutes to plug the outflow. I learned to live with the leeches of Borneo clinging to my skin, and would stop periodically to burn them off with a cigarette.

Walid's village, smaller than I anticipated, blended into the forest perfectly. Every structure was built of materials found within ten feet of entering the forest. I marveled at the orangutans that so easily coexisted with the villagers. Perched in the forest canopy, they spent the bulk of their time playing. I immediately grasped why the orangutans are considered kin and are called the "people of forest." Their warm, expressive eyes and their sweet nature made me want to call them brother.

The village buzzed with news of Walid's building project, and I was treated like a jungle diplomat. This was one large community, and I noticed that the children treated all adults as parents. Dinner consisted of a collection of baked roots and river fish loaded with powerful orange peppers. I had not slept in the dirt for some time and I lay awake most of the night thinking of Panama. The following day the men of the village assembled their tools while I played with the orangutans. This was great sport, for the orangutans had no fear of me. We were all three years old, playing with sticks in our big backyard.

At sunrise we headed east on foot. Since most of the men would be gone for months I was surprised at how little ceremony accompanied their departure. No one knew how long these men would be gone. Life in the rainforest is not determined by days but rather by seasons. There is no calendar. Laden with tools, these men of small stature possessed great strength and moved through the forest with the agility of panthers.

At midday we came upon a road where we found a corroded flatbed truck waiting for us. The road had been all but destroyed by the rains, and we often had to get out and push the truck through walls of mud. After crossing miles and miles of oil palms, we arrived in the tiny coastal town of Semporna. It was almost sunset and Ron, predictably, was in high spirits. We located the only hotel in Semporna and checked in.

The Dragon Inn was built over the water, which was unique on its own, but the spacing of the floorboards is what made this establishment interesting. Many gaps in the floor were large enough to swallow a human foot. Numerous planks were missing or loose. I felt as if I was walking on water as the ocean constantly penetrated the floor, lapping up over my feet and my soul.

I awoke to the sound of a floating city splashing by my room. Ron explained these were sea gypsies who spent their entire life on water and only came to land to bury their dead. I had never seen gypsies before. Tattered and filled with fear, they stared at me as if I were from another world. Their shanty wooden platforms looked anything but seaworthy, and they had few of the accoutrements of the floating villages I had seen in Cambodia. These people lived exclusively on the ocean and survived entirely by its bounty. They carried no live animals. Seeing the gypsies and their way of life convinced me that now I truly was at the end of the road.

Ron and I were met with bewilderment at every corner. Most

residents of Semporna had never seen a Caucasian. A simple town, Semporna consisted of a dozen or so small businesses and a long dock jutting into the sea. The gypsies had tied their floating city to the dock and were engaged in feverish bartering, trading octopus for palm oil. When I approached, all negotiations momentarily stopped until they determined I was not a threat. The gypsy children could not keep their eyes off of me.

The gypsies, master squatters, could sit for hours without their butts touching the ground. I assumed this was to avoid the filth of their floors and to keep a low center of gravity at sea. From what I could see, they rarely bathed and what little clothing they possessed was worn threadbare. This style of living had to be driven by deep superstition along with an innate paranoia of the land and its inhabitants.

Ron had secured several boats to transport the materials and the village men to the island. These hand-made wooden boats, all vibrantly painted, very long and very narrow, sat deep in the water and did not appear to be seaworthy in design. From the look in eyes of the boat captains, this was a serious crossing well out of their comfort zone. A half a mile out of Semporna, the ocean took on a shade of blue that only comes from clear deep water. These waters boiled with massive schools of tuna and dorado while pods of dolphins feasted on the bounty. Hundreds of seabirds joined the feeding frenzy and it was not hard to see how the gypsies survived in these waters.

At first sight Sipidan appeared to be no larger than a soccer field. The white sand and tiny patch of jungle leapt off of the infinite blue canvas of the Celebes Sea. Sipidan was a true seamount. Within twenty steps of the island's idyllic beach, a sheer wall of coral dropped suddenly into the deep. This jewel of an island was home to hundreds of sea turtles, and they scattered in all directions as we struck the beach

The captains were anxious, urging us to get the boats unloaded quickly. Walid explained why. In local legend, Sipidan is haunted by a giant scarlet octopus that will devour anyone who braves these waters. These men were seeking to limit their exposure to this mythical beast.

It was possible to circumnavigate the island in ten minutes by foot. The forty or so trees that filled the island's center were saturated with fruit bats each the size of a house cat. Perpetually hanging inverted, these creatures raised the hair on my neck as they droned on in a constant chorus of eerie squeals. Every time they took flight, I instinctively fell to the ground to avoid their two-meter wingspan. By far my least favorite visitors to Sipidan, however, were the sea snakes. Though docile and slow moving, these venomous banded serpents found refuge under everything I picked up.

As in Tortuguerro the first job was to build a dock. The village men were terrified of the ocean, so it fell to me to set the posts in the shallow reefs that led to the drop off. Coral was much more resistant than river silt, and it took me days to set the posts. I had to constantly pound the coral with a large metal bar to dig a footing.

The shallows were teeming with life as well as danger. Thousands of radiantly colored orange and purple fish filled the translucent waters. Sea turtles would pop up next to me as if they wished to shake my hand in a neighborly gesture. Perfectly camouflaged stonefish cleverly faded into the coral. These invisible fish sported a large thorn that could easily penetrate my shoes, delivering a fatal toxin. The tiny and deadly blue-ringed octopus would hide in crevices, keeping constant watch on my every move. The drop off was continually patrolled by hammerhead and reef sharks, and my pounding on the coral only drew them closer.

Living under tarps, we all worked from dawn to dusk. We spent the evenings eating rice and fish and consuming some sort of powerfully fermented fruit juice. At night the ocean creatures rose from the depths. Long chains of luminescent jelly fish put on a flashing neon light show that rivaled the stars above. The turtles struggled ashore to lay their eggs. We were visitors in this eco system, and I felt that we could be consumed at any time.

My apparent lack of fear of the ocean earned me the respect of the village men, but when Ron and I prepared to jump off of the dock in SCUBA gear they deemed us insane. Even Walid could be seen shaking his head. We had to time our dive carefully to avoid the currents that would surely take us out to sea. The steep wall dropped ceaselessly into the blue. It was encrusted with huge purple fans and multi-colored sponges that hid hundreds of species of fish. In the blue swam a school of barracuda so large it blocked the sunlight. Descending the wall, we came upon a school of two-hundred-pound parrot fish chewing on the coral. The sound of this sent shivers down my spine. At the corner I spotted thirty hammerhead sharks circling in their never-ending instinctual hunt.

Dropping deeper to avoid the sharks, we found an entrance to an underwater cave. As I started to swim into the narrow opening, Ron tugged at my fins. I turned to see him shaking his head profusely. In the distance I saw what appeared to be a school bus patrolling just off of the wall. I had never seen anything this large underwater and Ron, seeing my eyes widen, quickly spun around. She had to be forty feet long and it looked as if she could swallow a small car. Gracefully and slowly moving along the wall, she did not react to my presence or my touch. Adorned with a magnificent paint job of white spots on a gray background, she was careful not to hit me with her tail. I now knew why all divers consider the whale shark to be the most coveted encounter in the ocean.

Walid looked as if he had seen a ghost when we climbed up the dock. The men cheered in delight, and I was speechless. Ron gave me the "now you know why I am here" glance. We both knew that it would be next to impossible to top this dive.

Work on the resort continued and, between dives, I became the electrician. I preferred this work since it required planning and clear thinking. I had learned that too many days spent in total abnormality reduced my capacity for logical thought, and I needed the focus to hang on.

Every day Ron and I waited for the tide to peak, for this offered an hour or so window to dive. Although we never actually knew the time, the sea was our clock. We had learned that if we slowly rose from below, the barracuda would circle around until all we could see were their silver sides. Ron loved this game, but it always kept me on edge. On days when Ron was away, I would dive on my own. I soon learned to love the solitude and self-reliance of solo diving.

Every day I would swim by the opening to the cave and wonder what lurked inside. Ron had great respect for the dangers of cave diving, and I too had heard horror stories of divers stirring up so much silt they lost all orientation. But when a large turtle paddled into the cave, I had to follow. The constricted entrance opened into a cavern the size of a country schoolhouse. The beam of light coming from the entrance illuminated dozens of turtle carcasses lying in perfect symmetry. The currents that raged just outside the cave had not disturbed a bone for a hundred years. As a child, I had heard that elephants have a secret place that they go to die, and I now assumed the same of turtles.

When Ron returned from town with a newspaper, I saw that it was time to leave. I had no idea where the past fifty days had gone. Borneo was a land lost in time. I was living on the fringe of lunacy and if I did not keep moving I would be equally lost. I declined Ron's offer of payment knowing the experience was priceless.

STONE AGE

Anchored in Kota Kinabalu harbor, the Victoria looked inviting. I knew that the crew and especially the captain would help me re-enter the western world. Just as expected, I was welcomed aboard the ship and took my first shower in sixty days. For me a hot shower alone defines the western world.

The ocean had become my life, and I knew I would never stray far from it. For ten days we motored through Indonesia passing miles of reefs and lush volcanic islands. We were headed for Papua New Guinea, an island nation whose existence was unknown to me. The crew of the Victoria spoke ill of New Guinea, describing the aboriginal people as lawless and barbaric. The captain, however, described primitive people of fascinating cultures in stone-age dress, most of them discovered only thirty years ago. Two hours from Port Moresby we lost an engine. As we limped into port, I could sense the captain's frustration. Anyone seeking repairs in this port would be challenged. We all accepted our fate. We knew we would spend a month in Port Moresby.

Steaming hot, Port Moresby was the razor wire capital of the world. Even the simplest residence was appointed with a perimeter of impenetrable razor wire, confirming that no one here was to be trusted. Almost exclusively cinderblock and tin-roofed houses lined the streets, and everyone sized me up for the taking. Sensing that I was more likely to be mugged than killed, I would not go out at night.

Each day I joined the captain for the run to the airport in

hopes that the flight from Australia would bring engine parts for the Victoria. In this way I came to know most of the businessmen in New Guinea, as invariably they would all await the flight for critical supplies. It was sort of a club whose members had to have a sense of humor to survive the daily disappointment.

My favorite character was a stout, ruddy-faced gentleman named Bob. Of Australian descent, he had been in New Guinea for many years yet somehow had managed to maintain the principles and practices of his upbringing. I was not surprised to learn that he was a pilot who operated an air cargo company. He distributed medical supplies and other necessities throughout the country. We would pass the hours waiting for the flight discussing aviation in any form.

When Bob showed up at the dock one morning asking if I wanted to join him on a flight to the Highlands, I leapt at the opportunity. The airplane was familiar as it was the identical model that had crashed in Corcovado. Bob asked me what seat I wanted, and I requested the left. I was not surprised to find there was no checklist. Pilots like Bob were the checklist. I taxied us onto the runway and pushed the throttle forward, wondering if Bob was going to step in and take over. He never looked up.

"Three five zero," he said, indicating I should steer us north.

Being back in the air was like being home. Instantly my senses came alive, snapping me out of my doldrums. Below lay a blanket of green, tightly woven with trees and vines. For more than two hours I saw no roads and no signs of life I was thrilled to see that the runway in Mount Hagen had been recently paved and was fairly long. I had not shot a landing in almost a year and I needed those comforts.

Tying down the airplane, we were met by a local man in a tattered olive-green uniform with a large bone through his nose. He was the local representative of the government, and Bob dismissed him in an odd language that almost sounded like English. I suspected that this was as sophisticated as the Highlands of New Guinea would get.

After loading the cargo into a small truck, we bounced through the streets of Mount Hagen. This was the business center of the Highlands but, from what I could see, there was little business to be done. A large field of dirt served as the market where a hundred or so vendors were selling small collections of fruits and yams. Out of town the road worsened and we resigned ourselves to the slow pace. Bob explained that fifty thousand people occupy the Highlands speaking hundreds of languages and practicing dozens of religions.

We passed miles of tea fields with only an occasional village on the side of the road. Dropping into the Waghi Valley, we found ourselves instantly displaced ten thousand years in history. The collection of aboriginal people in traditional dress was staggering. I was no longer on the same planet. Before me stood men, women and children with faces and bodies painted in blues, yellows and reds, their heads topped with extravagant headdresses of the most beautiful feathers I had ever seen. Large bones penetrated their noses and heavy earrings dragged their earlobes down to their shoulders. Around their necks some of the women wore forty pounds of jewelry which hung down to their toes. The scene was impossible to digest and, for a moment, I was sure all this was a hallucination. One tribe painted every bone on their body, projecting a skeletal apparition that would give any child nightmares. Almost unrecognizable as humans, they all carried clubs, spears, bows and arrows leaving little doubt that tribal war was their world. This was a rare meeting of the tribes known as a sing sing.

We were carrying a camera for a British film crew that was documenting the event, and they were thrilled to see us. Bob and I stayed and watched the show in utter disbelief. The dances always mocked battle and demonstrated great bravery. Each and every culture was strikingly unique in its dress, dance, and language, and I marveled that so many micro cultures could coexist. The scene just kept getting more and more bizarre. One woman, her body painted in purple streaks with a snow-white face, wore a human wrist as a necklace. Though I had been told that cannibalism was no longer practiced in New Guinea, I knew it was not too far in the past.

It was the Mud Men who took the show. Their clay masks were caricatures of evil gargoyles so large they dwarfed their mud-slathered bodies. With fingernails half a foot long they crouched like tigers, their bows drawn taut. There was little doubt that I would surrender.

Our drive back to Hagen was quiet. My travels had taught me that I often do not have enough time to process all that I witness and experience. I knew I would be processing that afternoon for years to come. When we reached the airport, I was glad to see Bob jump in the left seat of the plane. At his core, he was a man of confidence, and I suspected I could learn much from this wanderer.

Bob was a stick and rudder pilot who survived on feel. The environment in which he operated defied rules and demanded interpretation. He rarely looked up and always knew where he was. He hit the first twenty feet of the dirt runway and we rolled out in Tari. High in the mountains the air in Tari was cool, a sensation I had not experienced in a year. Tari was gorgeous. Overlooking the spectacular jungle valley, I saw skies full of vividly colored birds I had not yet seen.

Upon our arrival, the Huli came out of the bush to investigate. The costume of the Huli Wigmen who inhabited Tari was magnificent. Wearing true grass skirts, their faces and bodies were painted a bright yellow with red highlights. They fit their environment perfectly, mimicking the color of the birds. The Huli all carried spears.

Bob and I climbed into what had to be the only truck in Tari and endured the hour's drive to the Huli Village. Bob was frustrated. His supply of fuel at the Tari airport had disappeared, and we were meeting with the Huli elders to seek its return. The village was surrounded by dozens of tiny gardens, mostly growing yams. Round stick-sided huts with thick roofs of palm circled the central meeting area. Most huts had a fire burning inside, leaving the center of their roofs black with soot.

When we arrived the village elders stood up and the children scattered, hiding in the nearby jungle. I could not help but smile as I watched Bob address this collection of brightly decorated diplomats. The tallest elder spoke pidgin, a morph of English that came from the coast and was used as the universal language for trading. From what I could surmise, Bob was praising them for their courage as he delivered medical supplies from the plane. I would have thought it smart to hold back the supplies to barter for the fuel, but I could see that in this world trust was foremost.

We were invited to sit on the log and soon the children crept out of the jungle and surrounded us. Though the children were very timid, I could tell by their faces that they were fascinated by me. They seemed eager to show me their world. Together we followed a trail that led to an extremely dense jungle which eventually opened up at the river. Crossing on a shaky bamboo suspension bridge, we arrived at a waterfall plummeting several hundred feet from the cliff above. Flocks of red parrots, numbering in the hundreds, filled the sky. Hornbills with four-foot wingspans would dive bomb us from the trees. It would be difficult to imagine a more beautiful place.

As we returned to the village, I could hear the drums beating. We arrived to find Bob freshly painted in yellow and red. The village was in the midst of a hair growing ceremony and the dance was feverish. All the dancers carried weapons and moved in unison. The ceremony stopped when they poured water on Bob's head. For the first time I heard laughter.

It was now time to prepare for the evening's feast. Like most cultures, they preferred me sitting down in an obvious act of submission. Each child brought their puppy or pig for my approval. Dinner consisted of yams and other roots which had steamed all day in banana leafs. Seated in a circle, we all shared the food spread before us. Yams were among my least favorite food, but I had to push them down in respect. The Huli go down with the sun, and I was ushered into one of the huts. I found it impossible to sleep as the hut reeked of soot and body odor. It was too cold to sleep outside, so I spent the night listening to the songbirds and insects.

At dawn we said a sincere goodbye, and the entire Huli village followed us to the truck. In the back was the barrel of fuel. Bob was careful not to take notice of its return. The deal had been struck and, from what I could ascertain, without conversation.

At the airport, we filled the tanks on the airplane and put the remainder of the fuel in back. On approach to the Port Moresby airport, I was disheartened to look over and not see the Victoria tied to the dock. I walked across the street and checked into the Gateway Hotel just as the fever hit. Soon the chills and shakes came, and I knew I was in for a long one. I had been very lucky since falling off Daisy, but I was due.

The days drifted into nights as I faded in and out of delirium. I recall my dreams being as surreal as the Highlands. Painted men in gruesome masks haunted me. I awoke five mornings later to find the maid taking my pulse. When my eyes popped open, she ran in terror as if I had risen from the dead. Surely now I would haunt her dreams.

I found Bob at the airport changing oil. He did not comment on my absence. Again, without looking up, he simply said he had some work for me. An Australian pilot who worked for Bob had been forced to land in the remote Sepik Region when he ran out of fuel. He had radioed his circumstance just before landing at a jungle airstrip called Timbunke but had not been heard from since.

Bob had flown over Timbunke and seen the airplane stuck in the middle of the airstrip. Neither he nor any other pilot could land here. Bob gave me the left seat, and we set a course for Wewak. On the way Bob told me that there would be a boat waiting for me at the river. He further explained that it would take five days by riverboat to get to Timbunke. On board were fuel and tools.

The Sepik River Valley was flat and contained a perpetual maze of rivers and tributaries. Wewak did not get much air traffic, and we had to clear children off of the runway with a low pass before landing. The moment we shut down the engine, we were surrounded by local people pressing their noses on the glass to get a look at our cargo. Bob dispersed the crowd by explaining we were missionaries doing God's work.

We loaded the boat and I was surprised to see Bob look up with concern as we departed. My guide was a young man with kind eyes that seemed to look through me. Semson was the baby the mule kicked, constantly distracted and barely responsive. He could sleep anywhere, anytime and as soon as he determined I could drive the boat, he slept often. His English was good and I could tell it all came from the Bible. The boat was familiar since it was almost identical to the riverboats in Asia, though more crudely carved. I was relieved to see that it had an Asian engine, one that was capable of taking us up the Sepik River for the next five days.

The rainforest canopy was so thick that no light touched the ground. All life seemed to be fighting for the sun, and it looked as if the vines would win. Just before sundown we arrived at a collection of stilt huts built on the river's edge. Twenty of so people were standing by the river, apparently drawn by the sound of our engine. Though they were not as colorfully decorated as the people of the Highlands, I knew I was still lost in the Stone Age.

Several of the villagers yanked me from the boat and dragged me to a hut set well away from the river. Inside a middle-aged man lay on the floor, shaking violently. He was tied up for his own safety. When Semson explained that I was not a doctor, the villagers became angry with me. Semson and I were sent fleeing to the river ducking stones.

Semson told me that there were two kinds of white men on this river – missionaries or doctors. Anyone could see I was not a missionary. It is a custom for the oldest son to eat the brains of his dead father in order to gain his wisdom. Unfortunately, this practice afflicts many a son with a fatal illness similar to Mad Cow Disease. The people of this village saw me as their last hope, and from what I could tell, I was. I understood their disappointment.

Completely unwelcome, we chose to continue up river by night until the rains obscured our vision. Tying off to a tree, we wrapped in tarps and pretended to sleep. The rain poured down the entire next day and the river began to run more swiftly. Our progress was sluggish, and the scenery never changed.

Late that afternoon we arrived at Semson's village. Set well back from the river, the buildings reminded me of those I had seen in Cambodia. Rectangular longhouses with steep thatched roofs were built on poles. The floors were well above the river level, leaving me to believe the Sepik was capable of significant floods. At the peak of each roof was a beautiful carving of a crocodile guarding each hut like a sentry. I was sure no one in this village knew or needed to know what decade it was.

The people of Semson's village looked alike; they wore little or no clothing and highlighted their cheekbones and ribs with pale yellow paint. They were master carvers and the collection of wooden drums, masks, and figurines were worthy of display in any museum. In the center of the village stood the apparatus for extracting food from a palm tree, a very labor intensive activity. Just the first step, stripping the bark and pounding the fibrous center to a pulp, took the bulk of the day.

Sago was a tasteless blend of sawdust and gruel, and I was tired of eating out of respect. I feared another fever and for sure I did not wish to contend with any illness in the Sepik. Refusing the second serving of sago that night, I was glad to see my hosts greet this gesture with laughter. Sago Palms filled the Sepik Region and I suspected the people ultimately resigned themselves to eating them out of necessity rather than choice. That night we slept family style on woven mats, hoping for the rain to stop.

It did not. The river was really flowing now, and we were lucky to gain any ground in the current. Semson said he had heard of a smaller river that would lead to Timbunke though neither he or nor anyone from his village had ever explored it. We both knew we did not have enough fuel to fight the Sepik upstream, so by default we turned east onto the tributary.

I was not sure if Semson was nervous or excited, but he chose not to nap that day. A mile in, the tributary turned to black water like I had seen in Tortuguerro. Black water always meant little current and our progress improved. Around midday we came upon some fisherman standing in their tiny carved canoes. Semson asked them where the river led and they said they had no idea. Most residents of the Sepik had canoes that could hold only three people. Journeys of more than a few miles from home were unheard of.

The tributary snaked in so many directions I had lost my bearings. The jungle canopy was so thick I could not even use the sun as a navigational reference. Sighting a village just before sunset, we decided to stop to ask about Timbunke, for we both lacked confidence in our decision. Before the boat came to a stop, I felt a spear pierce my chest. Total chaos erupted while the village women screamed, collected the children, and scattered. Semson stood stone faced. I could see fear in the eyes of the men which made them even more dangerous.

These men were naked, their bodies streaked with bright crimson paint on almost every bone. I maintained steady eye contact and asked Semson to explain that I had heard they were the strongest and bravest people on the river, and I wished to meet such men. This was met with nods of agreement. The oldest man started poking me to determine my authenticity, and I did not flinch. A few of the other men went through our belongings, marveling at the collection of tools. I decided to step ashore and was greeted with the raising of several more spears. I immediately sat down in the mud.

"They think you are an evil spirit," Semson said.

"Tell them that spirits do not bleed," I said as I pulled up my shirt.

The head villager stepped forward, touched my chest and rubbed my blood between his fingers. As I stood up, a few of the men smiled while others backed away in distrust. Semson asked if the river led to Timbunke and I was thrilled to see the men agree. They said that men from Timbunke had once passed this way and they believed it was a ten day journey. The head villager also warned of great danger, saying his brother went up river and never returned.

My heart was still hammering in my chest when I jumped in the boat and started the engine. I chose not to look back, knowing that that this encounter could have gone another way. I resolved to bypass any other villages on this river.

The river narrowed to the point that the jungle would scrape us from above and below, bringing our progress almost to a standstill. This was not a good sign as rivers narrow at their source. Then all at once the forest opened, and we saw we were at a convergence. The trees were full of cockatoos feeding on jungle fruit, and the sun shone directly above. Three rivers flowed in three different directions, and neither of us had a clue as to which to take. Observing that the river on the left flowed with more authority, we both knew it was our best call. Turning upstream I could see what the head villager meant. I saw the largest crocodiles I had ever seen. Twenty feet in length, they dwarfed all others I had encountered. Semson's eyes filled with fear as we passed. All life in the Sepik feared these prehistoric creatures.

Our fuel was disappearing quickly and we had no idea if we were on the right track. In aviation this is called V2 or decision speed, a critical point in time when the pilot must decide whether he is in or out. There was enough fuel to get back to Wewak but only if we turned back now. Semson's input was useless, for he was seeking advice from higher voices. I sensed my freedom was in Timbunke, so I kept going up river.

When the rains ceased, the heat came and there was not a breath of wind or a cloud in the sky. The sun and humidity were relentless. That night, tied up on the river, I drowned in my own sweat all the while swatting at legions of insects. I needed a break from the intense heat, and found one the next morning when we merged onto a larger river with many villages strewn across its banks. Using the engine to hold the boat against the current, I asked Semson to swim ashore and ask about Timbunke and see if there was any fuel. As I remained suspended in the middle of the river, some villagers rowed out to look at me. By now I was getting used to this. A smiling Semson soon returned saying Timbunke was just up the river, but there was no fuel.

The very short grass runway was surrounded by trees on three sides and fell off into the river. The airplane appeared intact. There was no sign of the Australian pilot, not even a note in the cockpit. I pulled the fuel strainer and not a drop came out. Surely he must have touched down in Timbunke without power. As I looked around, I realized this was a very impressive feat.

We carried enough fuel to get the airplane back to Port Moresby, but I knew I needed to give most of it to Semson for the boat. Scanning the chart in the cockpit, I determined that the town of Lae was an hour's flight away. I knew there was no fuel in Wewak but, from the size of the runway in Lae, I concluded they would have to have gas. We fueled the airplane and said our goodbyes at the river.

When Semson hugged me, we both started to cry. We knew we were only half way through this journey. The airplane started immediately and, as I taxied to the river's edge, I knew I had to summon the focus. Short field takeoffs always put a pilot on edge and this one offered little to no forgiveness. Clearing the trees by twenty feet, I was grateful to be low on fuel. With any more weight I might not have made it. At that very instant, I evolved ten thousand years.

Flying westerly, I observed that New Guinea transitioned from jungle to grasslands. Soon the ocean came into view. Everyone at the airport was surprised by the airplane's arrival but even more surprised to see me in the cockpit. I had not seen a reflection of myself in a week. I was covered in mud from head to toe. I downplayed my condition, not wishing to tell the Sepik story, and asked to purchase some fuel.

The men at this airport spoke excellent English, confirming that missionaries had been in Lae for some time. A teenage boy named Topo said they were expecting some fuel to arrive by boat in the next few days. This was news that I had almost anticipated. Topo gave me a ride to the hotel on his bicycle. He asked me many questions about who I was and where I came from. For the life of me, I could not answer.

I had been asleep for more than twelve hours when Topo knocked on the door. He informed me that the boat had not yet arrived, but I could see he had more on his mind. I invited him into the room and he asked questions about his country and what I had seen. As I described the people of the Highlands, he sat up straight, his eyes filled with curiosity. He had heard of such people but he had never seen them. Sensing my interest in New Guinea culture, he asked if I would like to meet his father. Considering my options that day, I said yes.

I borrowed a bicycle from the hotel and we rode through the dirt streets of Lae and then out into the hills past town. Stopping at a trail, we left our bicycles on the ground and I followed Topo, the two of us stomping our way through grass over six feet tall. At the top of the mountain was Topo's father. Tied in a sitting position, he had been mummified from smoke. Next to him were six other smoked relatives resembling a New Guinea version of the Last Supper. Topo explained that it was his people's belief that they could come to this place and seek wisdom from their forefathers who were still with them.

I was saturated. Emotionally done. I knew it was time to leave this indescribable corner of the world before it haunted me forever.

Bob paid me well and asked no questions. This was his way of showing respect. He could see it was time for me to go, and he gave me the name of a man at the port who could get me on a ship. It is not possible to say goodbye to men like Bob. I just figured next time we would pick up where we left off.

THE DARK CONTINENT

The Jambo was in total disrepair. Not an hour of maintenance had been performed in a decade on this East African tramp steamer. Despite the despicable conditions, her crew was full of laughter and ebullience. I had to assume that life at home was more challenging for these sailors than the day to day drudgery on the Jambo. It was to be a long crossing to East Africa, and I decided to make the best of the situation.

The captain had total authority and, from what I could tell, there was no second in command. He shook my hand as I boarded.

"This should be most entertaining," he said in perfect Queen's English, giving me the once over with an expression of amusement.

The Jambo barely made way, and the cargo was unknown. The crew lived in the moment and sought happiness in every corner. I spent much of the time studying the captain's charts of the Indian Ocean, intrigued by remote islands we would be passing. He would often comment that the difference between me and the rest of the crew is I wanted to know where we were going. Nobody worked too hard on the Jambo.

I could smell Mombassa from twenty miles out to sea. The dry season had fouled the waters of the port. Ripe with aromas, both natural and unnatural, this Kenyan coastal city nevertheless looked like Shangri La to me. I was through with ships. The life of a sailor was not for me, and I vowed to fly out of Africa regardless of the price.

The port was rough, as most ports are. I caught a ride with one of the crew who warned me that it was not safe to walk. A river divided Mombassa and all traffic waited for the next barge, which crossed every ten minutes. Many businesses thrived at this convergence since they had captive customers. In the queue were hundreds of dilapidated trucks and tractors. All passenger vehicles and busses were so overloaded that heads, arms, shoulders, and whole torsos protruded from the doors and windows. An unceasing line of local people pedaled cashews and cold beer while passengers waited for the crossing. The fervor, noise and aromas were intense.

I was dropped off at the Reef Hotel and checked in. I would not be able to afford a long stay at this beach resort, so I decided to fully enjoy what time I had. I had not been in a swimming pool for months, and again I needed the chlorine to help rid me of the insect bites that remained from New Guinea.

In the bar that night I found an animated young man sitting in what I assumed was his usual corner. With the lively eyes of an adventurer and a quick wit, Ranjit radiated charisma and exuded enthusiasm. Surely he had to be the brightest light on the coast. We exchanged stories well into the night and I do not recall the walk back to my room.

It took more than an hour's swim in the warm Indian Ocean to shake the night before. Mid morning I found Ranjit sitting in the shade by the pool. The conversation picked up where we left off, and as usual his humor was spot on. Although he had been born in East Africa, he had been schooled in London and California. He was a citizen of the world. A free diver, Ranjit had spent much of his childhood spear fishing with his father in the remote islands off of Northern Tanzania. We shared a passion for the ocean, and we vowed to dive together one day.

The Mombassa train station was wedged. The train to Nairobi

only came once a day and there were far more passengers than seats. The tent city surrounding the train station suggested many had been waiting for weeks. Undaunted, Ranjit's assistant cut through the crowd and found me a seat in front. I was seeking employment as a pilot, and I had been told that the best opportunity would be with the safari companies based out of Nairobi.

Away from the coast, Kenya turned desert dry. Miles of scattered acacia trees somehow thrived in dead grasses and clay. No travel in Africa is ever dull. In the distance giraffes chewed on the treetops while hundreds of zebras and wildebeests grazed on the land. Hyenas patrolled the railroad tracks seeking road kill. Certainly no person would last long on foot. The entire landscape seemed to be in a constant state of alert as if at any moment a herd of animals might stampede. I was captivated.

Nairobi station made Mombassa look like a walk in the park. The moment the door opened packs of frenzied travelers swarmed into the cabin nudging those of us bound for Nairobi out of the windows. Crossing back over the tracks, I was surprised to hear someone call my name. A smartly dressed man approached and shook my hand.

"Ranjit called," he said.

Right away I knew Shiban was a soldier; his form of respect had to have been drilled into him. He spoke few words and asked me no questions as we drove into the heart of this sprawling, wretchedly poor city. Nairobi lacked even the thinnest veneer of charm. An industrial center, the air was thick with pollution. At the city's edge were the huge scrap yards that thousands called home.

When we arrived at Pollman Safaris yard, I could see that they were loading for at least fourteen nights in the bush. I was offered a job on the expedition and signed on without hesitation. As a child I had always dreamed of an African safari. Excited by my good fortune, I decided to explore the streets of Nairobi.

The streets of Nairobi offered the same sensory overload as Asia. Unlike Asia, however, desperation filled the air. A bone thin child approached me with his hand out. The instant I reached into my pocket, dozens of children appeared out of nowhere and surrounded me, all begging for money. I had to keep moving continuously as hordes of children followed me constantly pleading. But it was the disease that was entirely unavoidable. A man with a tumor the size of a football growing from the side of his head sat on the corner holding a cup. A woman with legs the size of her torso was suffering from Elephantiasis. Ultimately it was the lepers wrapped in thin bloody cloth who finally drove me back to Pollmans.

Returning to the yard I was introduced to the four Americans who would be joining the safari. They were photographers for a famous magazine, and they were very excited about the upcoming adventure. I could see Shiban did not take to these four. Before sunrise we departed for the Mara in three Land Rovers, all towing trailers. The Maasai Mara occupies the northern tip of the vast Serengeti plains and we were seeking to catch the Great Migration. Each year literally hundreds of thousands of zebra and wildebeest chase the rains to the north in search of green grass. The majority of predators in East Africa inevitably join this annual migration delivering the ultimate in raw nature.

At first I found it hard to believe that we could get so close to so many animals. All the animals seemed indifferent to our presence, making us feel almost invisible. We came so close to a pride of lions I could smell their breath. Forty elephants passed so near they caused the ground to vibrate underneath our tires. The abundance of wildlife was overwhelming. In any direction I turned, I saw as many as ten different species of animals, always in great numbers. All were alert to the inevitable pending attack.

It was easy to buy into this fear, and soon I felt equally vulnerable.

"This is insane," I thought as we built the camp overlooking the Mara River. Every animal, bird and insect survives on this river and surely they all would invade our tents. The sounds of the night cut straight to my soul. The roars and howls raised the hair on my neck, reminding me that I was now part of the food chain.

With the morning sun the animals came like ants, first in little black lines from a distance until tens of thousands lined the banks of the Mara River. They had to drink, and we all knew it. The wildebeests were the first to go in. I was unclear if they were the bravest or the dumbest, but soon hundreds of other animals followed. The very moment that even one wildebeest became spooked, the others exploded in all directions, fleeing for their lives. This was real theater.

I thought it would be the crocodiles that made the first kill, but it was the lions. By the time we arrived at the scene, three lions were disemboweling a buffalo. True carnage was strewn in all directions and the smell was intolerable. No one wondered what the buffalo had for breakfast as it was hanging off the lions' bloody manes. Having consumed their fill, the lions rolled on their backs obviously stoned on the kill. The photographers loved this. I just looked at my feet and waited for it to end.

In the afternoon we crossed into Tanzania, foregoing the immigration process. This was critical, as I did not possess either a passport or a visa. I was working as a liaison for the photographers fielding all of their many requests. Shiban was happy not to have to deal with the Americans, and I soon gained his respect.

It was midday when we arrived at Lake Manyara. This beautiful region was adorned with trees and shrubs in stark contrast to the endless naked plains we had crossed. Baboons thrived in Manyara, often occupying the dirt road to the point of forcing us to stop. Baby giraffes chewed on the trees while infant baboons watched in fascination. The lake was filled with thousands of flamingos. As I walked along the lake's edge, the whole world seemed to be engulfed in shades of iridescent pink. When these magnificent birds took flight, I felt as if I were flying with them though I was merely standing below staring in awe.

After the camp was built I took a walk despite Shiban's protest. A walk in Africa is like no other. Though I had traversed many other wild regions of the world, a simple stroll in Africa carried the greatest risk. Behind every bush or in any field of tall grass violent death lurked. My senses peaked and my mind wandered. I never felt more vulnerable, and I never felt more alive.

As on an Asian sidewalk, I had to know precisely where I would take my next step while occasionally glancing up at the horizon. If I moved carefully enough and did not make eye contact, I could get within inches of adult giraffes. Their enormous size helped assure their survival and when they were in groups of ten or more, they feared nothing. Of all the animals in Africa these were the most impressive. Their design was brilliant, their majesty unmistakable. A giraffe in full run was as beautiful and ungainly a sight as nature could offer.

It was the hippos that most objected to my presence. Their protests were direct and I knew exactly what they were saying. Anything short of an immediate departure would be met head on with surprising speed and vigor. These are the most feared animals in Africa and I could see exactly why. Despite the peaking of my primal instincts, I felt a sense of calm in Manyara beyond anything I can explain.

The photographers were thrilled to see the rim of Ngorongoro Crater in the distance. As we parked on the rim, I could see why. A sheer drop of two thousand feet opened into a carpet of green grass that ran thirty miles to the other side. A perfect circle, this had to be the byproduct of a massive volcanic explosion. Tens of thousands of animals dotted the landscape and from what I could tell there was no way in or out.

At sunrise we started down the switch back road and descended into the crater. A thousand feet below the rim we entered into a gray ground fog so thick we could barely see. I was dispatched to walk the edge of the narrow dirt road and guide the Land Rovers down. I had difficulty seeing my feet, much less the edge of the road, and I felt my heart hammering through my shirt. Over the sound of the engines, I could hear the cries of hyenas in the midst of a kill. The road dropped suddenly. An hour flew by in minutes.

On the crater floor we had no choice but to wait. There were no roads in Ngorongoro, and we had to see in order to move. The gray was truly eerie. My sense of sound heightened to where I could hear every breath of the thousands of unknown animals that surrounded me. Occasionally the silhouette of a buffalo, coming out of nowhere, would disrupt this bizarre setting. By mid morning the fog was lifting, and the vibration of elephants on the move rocked the truck. They had to be very close, but we could not see them. Totally out of character, Shiban became nervous and started the engine. Although indifferent to the lions, Shiban had a healthy fear of elephants that I trust came from experience.

Out of the mist, he charged like a runaway locomotive. Easily twenty feet tall, he sported one massive tusk. He saw us as a threat and was acting on it. Shiban moved quickly and the chase was on. As we bounced across the grass, flying blind, all I could think of was Chinchoro Lagoon. Animals the size of our truck were fleeing in all directions and the bull elephant was only a few feet from our flank. Shiban swerved to avoid a rock and all at once the tusk shattered the back window.

Without warning, we broke into full sunlight and the chase was over as the elephant turned away. When we stopped to inspect the damage, I marveled at the beauty of the crater floor.

Majestic cliffs marked every corner of the horizon. This crater was a bowl of life. In any direction I could see dozens of different species of animals all commingling in relative distrust. We spent that afternoon photographing rhinos constantly being harassed by ostriches. These birds stood well above our Land Rovers and often attacked us, snapping their beaks through the open roof. Climbing out of the crater at sundown, I felt fortunate to have survived another day in East Africa.

The Serengeti plains stretched on forever only occasionally broken by odd large rock outcroppings. These outcroppings were invariably the habitat of cheetahs or lions. They used the rocks as vantage points in their perpetual pursuit of the kill. On some days we would see the Maasai herding cows in the distance. Dressed in bright red, the Maasai were truly nomadic people who were never seen without their spears.

Born survivors, the Maasai surrounded their villages with circular fences of eight foot tall timbers. The cows enjoyed the identical comforts of the children. Unlike Ngorongoro, most animals segregated in the Serengeti and found safety in large numbers. On constant look out, they never relaxed. This was in direct contrast to the animals of the rainforest who spent the bulk of their time resting in the afternoon's heat. Here the tension in the air was palpable as every animal was hard-wired to embrace that anxiety. Everyone one of us knew it was just a matter of time. Nothing dies from natural causes in the Serengeti; sooner or later, everything gets eaten.

We crossed the Serengeti for several days. Each night brought visitors to our camp. The lions were just curious but always confined us to our tents. The hyenas were the most intrepid. All the noise or harassment we could muster did not deter them, and we often spent most of the night throwing sticks while they constantly sought our blindside.

We arrived at the Rufiji River in the heat of the afternoon. As much as I longed for bath, I knew no river in Africa was safe for swimming. We inflated our rafts and lashed in our last supplies. We were low on food and water and I knew the hope of a sixty-mile run of this river were thin. Shiban and his friends had proven themselves very competent on land, but I could see they were not river people. I suspected they were in well over their heads. Pulling Shiban to the side, I asked if anyone here had run the river before. He hesitated to answer.

"No," he finally offered in a low voice.

The Rufiji was calm when we put in and I hoped it would remain that way. The riverbanks were filled with thousands of birds offering a deafening chorus of squawks. Sensing everyone's hesitation, I pushed off first in the supply raft and headed for the middle of the river. The banks of this river were certain to be full of predators.

It felt good to be back on the water, though odd to be in a western man's raft. At every bend in the river, we encountered another large collection of animals totally surprised by our presence. The animals in this remote area of southern Tanzania were not accustomed to humans and often reacted to our intrusion with aggression. Elephants roared in protest and the crocodiles slipped into the murky river at the first sight of us. Every slack water section of the river was full of hippos, and they defended their territory passionately. This river belonged to the animals.

The sun was low and we needed to find a place to set camp. For the last hour, the riverbanks had been too steep to climb, and we soon accepted the reality that we would be seeking shelter in the dark. Certainly this was a river no one ran at night. A nearly full moon reflected every eye in the river, and there were many. My raft was heavier than the others, and I soon started to lag behind. The river was sucking me in and my mind started to wander to thoughts of rivers past.

The calm was setting in when I heard Shiban yelling in Swahili. I could sense urgency in his voice. Turning the corner, I could see that the river was saturated with hippos. The other rafts had made it through though not without stirring up a ruckus. Hippopotamus teeth are very impressive, even more so on a moonlit night. I was half way through when I felt the raft deflate from the bite. Instinctually I climbed to the top of the supplies only to view a gaping hole in my raft. I had maybe a minute. The moment I cleared the hippos, I dove in and headed for the north bank. The water felt wonderful, and I fell into my survival state of mind: time stops and my mind overloads, I breathe like a machine and operate purely on instincts without the option of intellectual override.

When I reached the riverbank, I sat there for an hour trying to regain my mind. But nothing sits in Africa, especially at night, so soon I started down river. I was rattled and sure to be fodder. I moved recklessly and ignored the shadows moving around me until it was too late. The unmistakable chortle of hyenas filled the night. Hyenas survive by persistence and I knew I was no match. Running to the river's edge, I dove in and swam across to the southern side. I spent the rest of the night sitting motionless in the tall grass, like every other animal in Africa.

With the sun always comes hope, but this morning brought very little. I knew I was in real trouble. No man lives on this stretch of the river and I was on my own. It was midday when I broke down and drank from the river. Water is the very source of life, and I would not survive without it. At least this was my justification for what I knew was an ill-fated decision. The cramping began that night as I lay in the grass shaking. The fevers broke in minutes followed by intense chills. The following morning I made it to the shade and fell into delirium.

Their voices had to be a dream. All I could see was red. A wet rag dampened my forehead, and she was fanning me with her dress. Her eyes were soft and gentle, and I trusted her instantly. The mud hut was dark and the beam of light that came from the tiny window was filled with smoke and dust. A large cow slept on the dirt floor consuming half of the floor space.

Leva wore a dark blue dress with amber and ruby colored beads covering her neck. Her earrings draped down to her shoulders, and her smile was genuine. Just over five feet tall, she carried herself with the grace and the confidence of a born survivor. I was too weak to sit up as she fed me cow's milk. I would wake every few hours to the sound of children playing and then slip back into delirium, hopelessly lost in a daydream.

I was startled awake in the early morning by the sound of a cow screaming. I could see it was sunrise, but I was unable to get up. My fever was burning and my clothes were soaked. Leva was shooing the children away from the window while they were trying to sneak a peek at the stranger in their midst. Two more days disappeared before I had the strength to sit up. Looking out the window, I could see Leva playing games with the children. She seemed to possess authority in her community and was obviously loved by all.

The children helped me to my feet as I stepped out of hut into the streaming sunlight. The perimeter of the outpost was built of strong timbers buried vertically into the rock hard clay. Six tiny huts made of mud and dung were half the height of most of the men. Maybe thirty in total, including cows, lived in this bush fortress. There was no mistaking that the Maasai lived identically as the animals, in constant anticipation of the attack. At times the flies were so thick they obscured the horizon. Perpetual earth tones formed a perfect backdrop for the Maasai's vibrant dress. The men, stoic, strong and proud, viewed my arrival with indifference. In Africa each species must look out for its own. Nobody survives as an individual. Individuality comes well after hunger and thirst.

The Maasai were real people with real problems. With absolutely no sense of entitlement, they embraced even the smallest gifts. Their energy was uplifting, and everybody in this small tribe smiled. Communication was difficult, but then no one asked questions. Their favorite food was a mix of cow's blood and cow's milk. This less than attractive concoction would spill out of their mouths and dribble freely down their chins. The sole daily entertainment consisted of five men wrestling a cow to the ground and letting its blood. It was a fair fight, and often the cow would win.

Leva had two young sons, and she cared for them impeccably. From what I could gather, their father had gone hunting and never returned. Leva had accepted me as her third child and cared for me equally as well. But I was on the mend, and again it was time for me to move. Leva knew this, and her tears flowed openly. Before I left, she handed me a spear and a piece of torn cloth with a single sentence written in Swahili on it.

I had survived the past days on cow's milk alone and was bone thin. My escort was a lanky teenager who knew his backyard well. I never heard his feet touch the ground, and he saw everything without moving his eyes. We walked like brothers for two hours before we came upon a dirt road. He pointed to the east and turned to walk away. I stopped him with a touch on his shoulder and gave him my spear. We both laughed knowing the spear was useless to me. I would have never made it out of the Serengeti without these kind people.

I followed the road for a few hours growing accustomed to passing elephants and giraffes grazing by the side of the road.

Totally on the edge, I was getting mentally prepared for another night in the bush when, like a mirage, a battered yellow truck came hurtling out of the dust. Heavily overloaded, I could see its abundant cargo hanging over the sides. Screeching to a halt, the truck raised a dust cloud so thick I choked. There was only room to stand on the rear bumper and I was greeted with roars of laughter by twenty or more men hanging on to any available perch. I soon learned why the bumper was available as a constant cloud of black engine exhaust washed over my face. The truck was so burdened that it had no suspension, and my feet would bounce into the air at the slightest bump in the road. I was still very weak and it took all my strength to hang on.

Eventually the road joined the river and opened into miles and miles of mangrove. I knew the mangrove would lead to the sea, and soon I could smell the salt in the air from the brackish water. The road ended at the mouth of the river delta. Dozens of small wooden fishing boats were tied to the mangrove roots. A short wooden dock tilted into the water. The tattered tarps of the scattered tent camps offered little protection from the pouring rain. The rain was heaven sent and offered my first shower in a month. I spent that night in the forest thinking of Sirena.

I was thrilled to hear English being spoken as the crew unloaded spices at the river's edge. In total disrepair, the fifty-year-old supply boat complemented the scene perfectly. The captain, tall and imperious, ruled like a prison warden. Captain Jacob was constantly preoccupied. Nothing received his full attention. Incredibly fit, it was clear that he had scratched his way to the top. I professed my competence at sea, and he inspected my hands before sending me below.

We put to sea in the late afternoon with the dolphins at our bow. Looking over my shoulder, I felt the weight of predation lifting from my mind, knowing I was fortunate to be here at all. I spent the next four days in the engine room lost in gear oil and contemplation.

LOST AT SEA

Ten miles from Zanzibar, I caught the scent of cloves in the wind. Citadels overlooked this city, each topped with an ornate dome. I could hear the Muslim call to prayer echoing from the city as we docked in the Stonetown harbor. A fortress city, this aptly named town was truly made of stone. It was the doors I found most remarkable. Masterfully crafted intricate designs were meticulously carved out of hard wood. Many of these exquisite doors had weathered several hundred years. I stopped to marvel at each one as I navigated the endless maze of narrow, congested streets. Everywhere incense burned, and I could not see any woman's face.

The town center opened into a large market. In a moment, I was displaced to the twelfth century. Covered from head to toe in heavy black cloth, women sold vegetables in the midday sun. Buckets of spices were displayed on every corner as mangos and bananas rotted in the sun. The collection of spices numbered in the hundreds as they had come from all over Africa. Aromas of cardamom, nutmeg, and cloves filled the air. Zanzibar was a trading post, and everyone was a merchant.

Toward sunset, I wandered back to the harbor. The waterfront was filled with the triangular sails of the traditional Dhow. Looking much like pirate ships, these sturdy wooden ships had sailed the African coast for centuries. On the waterfront, I spotted several westerners drinking at the bar of the Tembo Hotel. As with the rest of Zanzibar, the bar contained a cosmopolitan mix of people.

When the conversations predictably turned to what brought me to Zanzibar, I just replied "long story." I enjoyed the company of these strangers, as well as a few drinks, before I decided to spend half of my net worth on a room and a shower. I had not seen a mirror in months and once again I did not recognize myself in the reflection. I was lost and very unsure of my next move. I knew it was time to go home, but I no longer was sure where that was.

After sleeping well into the afternoon, I meandered through the streets of Stonetown, totally lost. Coming upon a small beach I swam in the blue water for over an hour, foregoing my next decision. As always the ocean absorbed me and soon my mind wandered freely. I struggled to overcome the lingering effects of the Serengeti. The people of Zanzibar paid me little attention, proving this truly to be an island of transients. Passing the pier on the way back to the Tembo, I reaffirmed my vow never to live below deck again.

I did not even question finding Ranjit at the Tembo bar. Asia had taught me to accept this as destiny. As usual, his energy was captivating and soon we were talking well into the night. Ranjit's stories of exploring the Zaire River as a child rang in my ear, confirming that I would travel deeper into the Dark Continent.

The next morning I was surprised to awaken on a Dhow. Built of hardwood timbers, the Ghanima was well past her prime. Her decks were strewn with laundry baskets of food and supplies. Dozens of live chickens scrambled about trying to avoid all the other creatures. The foul aroma forced all but the most unfortunate to flee to the deck above.

Boasting a high back captain's deck, the timeless Ghanima, a beautifully crafted ship, sported windows worthy of a cathedral. I was introduced to the crew by an exuberant young boy named Danji. I guessed him to be seven years old, but he carried himself with a maturity well beyond his years, his soft eyes suggesting he was an orphan who had been caring for himself most of his short life. His smile could light the night, and he possessed a confidence that comes from accepting fate. Somehow I felt that Danji was ultimately in charge.

Captain Beech, a stalwart physical specimen, stood on the stern, staring right through me. I had not seen eyes like his since Ian's, and immediately I knew he was living on the very precipice of sanity. Beech ruled with an iron fist and all of us considered him as unpredictable as a rabid dog. Ranjit knew this and handled Beech with authority, demonstrating his amazing ability to cross the class distinctions of Africa. I was thrilled to see dive gear lumped in the back corner.

Untying from the pier, we drifted into the outgoing tide. The raising of the sails had little to do with mechanics and more to do with tradition. Barefooted, these seafarers danced in unison converting the Ghanima into a hundred foot drum. The beat was mesmerizing, running straight through my feet into my mind. Their medieval chants echoed across the deck as we picked up a north wind. Seeking forgiveness, these men knew that every crossing could be their last. I had come to learn that fearing the ocean was part of being a sailor, especially since few sailors could swim.

Ranjit and Beech were screaming at each other in Swahili when I decided to join them at the only table on the Ghanima. Beech wanted nothing to do with diving, arguing that it would be our certain death. Oblivious to Beech's concerns, Ranjit was explaining how he was to follow us once we were underwater. Just as they were about to reach détente, the cook threw down a live chicken and chopped its head off. Splattered with blood, Beech continued to state his objections without even acknowledging the death of the fowl. In Africa, death was part of everyone's daily lives.

The winds were soft and the crossing to Pemba took days. Unaware of Dhow protocol, I found myself sleeping below as the crew took all available deck space. The smell of two hundreds years of bilge forced me to hang my head out of the window seeking fresh air in a futile attempt to sleep. Around midnight I gave up and climbed on deck. Beech lay catatonic on the deck with his eyes wide open. I had never seen anyone or anything sleep with eyes open, and I longed for normality.

With the sun came dolphins by the hundreds, momentarily transporting me back to Baja. Ranjit threw me a mask and we dove in. I could only compare the frenzy of bodies rocketing by to rush hour in Bangkok. The noise was deafening as the ocean filled with grunts, clicks and incessant splashing. I could reach out and touch the dolphins as they passed by; their numbers were so large they created a current that pulled us out to sea. Climbing back on the Ghanima, Ranjit and I were speechless, stupefied by what we had just witnessed.

Crossing the southern point of Pemba Islands, we were greeted by a dozen or more fishermen in small hand-carved wooden canoes. In lieu of sails they would hold up broken tree branches to catch the wind. From what I could see, the fishing was excellent; many had caught sailfish as large as their canoes.

The western side of Pemba was lined with spotless white beaches devoid of footprints. When we dropped anchor, Danji and I dove in to explore. The sand was the finest I had ever felt. I likened it to walking on fresh snow. Seashells that would sell for fifty dollars in America littered the beach. Danji and I compared our finds and soon I, too, was seven years old. At the beach, the child in Danji came to life. I suspected his daily life left little time for play.

Swimming back to the Ghanima, I could hear the compressor running. The familiar clank of scuba tanks started my heart racing. I was certain that few people had dived these islands and, from what I had seen, marine life thrived in this area of the Indian Ocean. The crew surrounded us, gawking in disbelief, as we put the regulators in our mouths. In their minds they were looking at dead men.

The water was warm and clear as we dropped down the wall. The incoming current was ripping and soon we were on a roller coaster ride through the pass. As the pass widened, we shot over a school of the largest hammerheads I had ever seen. Once on the inside, the current stopped and we swam toward the reef in the center of the pass. In the distance they looked like a squadron of aircraft flying toward us in perfect formation. The ocean went dark when they crossed over my head. Their massive bodies blocked all sunlight. Easily twenty feet across these giants floated through the ocean with the ease of a butterfly. We sat in the sand watching the mantas dance until we were out of air. Breaking the surface, I was thrilled to see Danji's smiling face. Beech had done as Ranjit asked, and the Ghanima was there to recover us.

We anchored next to the reef and while waiting for the outgoing tide spent the afternoon watching the mantas jump in the lagoon. Danji was terrified of the mantas and would scream curses in Swahili every time one came near the boat. Ranjit was pumped and paced the deck in anticipation. The plan was simple. Beech would meet us on the outside pass and we would drift the outgoing current through the pass.

Jumping off of the back of the Ghanima, I knew we needed to get deep fast to avoid the strongest currents. At ninety feet I realized I was alone. Hanging onto the wall, I felt my head start to spin. Everything went black. When my vision returned I started for the surface. The moment I let go of the wall, the current caught me and I was sucked into the middle of the pass. Every few feet of ascent caused a room-spinning head rush, and I lost all orientation.

I could taste the diesel in my air. Time ceased as I worked my way to the surface while the world spun beyond control.

Breaking the surface, I spit out my regulator and rolled onto my back. The seas were large so I knew I was well outside the pass. In the fresh air my mind returned long before my vision, but it must have been an hour before I realized that I was adrift. The chances of being rescued in Pemba were thin, and I entered a sublime state of acceptance, beyond hope or denial. My fate was no longer in my control, and I would only survive on the kindness of strangers.

Six-foot high seas obscured the horizon but I could tell the sun would be setting soon. I knew the birds hovering above meant trouble as the oceanic sharks would soon follow. Oceanics wander the open sea in constant search of food and are reputed to eat anything and everything passionately. My stomach clenched as they circled.

Though I had learned not to fear sharks, these predatory specimens terrified me. The sharks opted to approach from my blindside, but a kick to their heads would send them darting into the blue. I was drawing a crowd when I heard the ruckus coming out of the sun. Thirty or forty of them approaching from all directions sent the sharks deep. Protecting me like one of their own, the dolphins chased the sharks even deeper. I was unsure if this attack was conducted on my behalf or was just part of an ongoing open ocean war. I knew that surviving the night would be a miracle. With the darkness came resignation. I was a prisoner. My dreams seeped through my pores.

LIFE'S LESSONS

At first light I spotted a mast in the distance. I was sure it was an illusion until I heard the joyous screams of Danji. Beech pulled me across the railing with one hand, then walked away mumbling in Swahili. Danji helped me out of my dive gear and gave me a big hug. After drinking a gallon of water, I climbed below and fell asleep oblivious to the odors.

When I awoke later that night, I found Danji and Beech sitting at the table. No one else was onboard. I could see myself in the reflection of Beech's eyes and realized that another week in Africa would find me equally unhinged. Danji was nervous and pointed to the empty rum bottle. Sensing his fear, I picked him up and carried him to his bed. I promised him we would collect shells in the morning, and we both fell asleep under the stars.

It must have been three in the morning when Beech began screaming like a banshee. Chopping the anchor rope free, he began running back and forth like a caged mongoose. When I tried to stop him from hoisting the sail, he effortlessly threw me to the deck. No one sails through Pemba at night and nobody knew this better than Captain Beech. Moments later we struck the reef, caving the bow of the Ghanima.

She went down in moments and Beech could not swim. I grabbed him around the neck and pulled him to the reef cutting us both to shreds on the razor sharp coral. Danji was already standing on the reef in a foot of water. I hoisted Danji up and put him on my shoulders as we all stood motionless staring at the moon like three lost children. By midnight the rain began to pelt us and the water rose above my waist. As with most life in the ocean, we waited for sunrise and the promise it brings. Danji squeezed my neck with his legs. Beech was absent. These two needed me and I could not help but recognize the irony, for they had just saved me.

At daybreak I could see islands a few miles away. Given the right tide, I knew Danji and I could make the swim, but we would have to abandon Beech. Since Beech had not abandoned me, this was not an option. Then through the morning mist came a canoe. He had come to investigate and showed no surprise at finding us standing there. Emaciated and appearing to be at least eighty years old, he, like us, was well beyond the moment. His canoe was twelve feet long, and the hammerhead he had caught was four feet longer. This impressive fish was weighting his boat to just above the waterline. Danji pleaded with him to save us, but I could see he was not going to relinquish his catch. This had to be the negotiation of the century. Everyone and everything in Africa contended almost exclusively with hunger and thirst. Self-preservation always took precedence. This was universally understood and carried neither obligation nor guilt. In Africa, Darwin had it right.

The old man explained that the shark would feed his village for a week, and his people all depended on him for life. Sensing his pride, I asked Danji to explain we too had family awaiting our return and surely they would not survive without us. He did not buy this as anyone could see the three of us were orphans and surely victims of our own devices. The laws of survival prevailed, and the old man raised his tree branch to catch the wind. I urged Danji to tell the old man that if he were to take us to the island, I would feed his village for a month. Looking into my eyes for well over a minute, he eventually nodded in agreement. I was not sure if his decision was based on our circumstance or what he saw in my eyes. It took all of us to get the shark out of the canoe. I guessed it to weigh six hundred pounds. Watching the shark drift off of the reef, the old man touched my shoulder, confirming our deal.

The boat sat heavy in the water, slowing us to a snail's pace. I could only question how life had brought the four of us together, and I longed for a camera. Danji's smile returned as did Beech's mumbling. I just sat in the boat wondering how I was going to feed his village for a month.

By midday we pulled the canoe onto the beach and started walking inland. It was hot and the bush was thick. An hour later we came upon a dirt road, and the old man pointed north. Walking like brothers we did not speak, each of us understanding that struggle finds common ground. An hour before sunset we arrived in Wete Town. Thirty or forty concrete structures filled the dirt streets all in varying states of construction. A mountain of cloves lay drying in the sun, and a few women sat in the dirt selling over-ripe fruits. The waterfront was strewn with Dhow carcasses and from what I could see there was little business being done.

Our arrival was met with fascination and soon many local people surrounded us, speculating on our presence. Out of the crowd a squat gentlemen approached me speaking clearly understandable English. He exuded authority, and everyone moved to give him room. I was getting ready to tell him my story when he asked for my passport. My laughing did not help matters as I attempted to explain that I was a sailor from Mombassa and did not need a passport.

The Wete jail was small and clean. A perfectly carved wooden door opened into four concrete walls with a view of the town center. I was sure I was not in serious trouble as the mothers allowed their children to peek at me through the door. The likelihood of anyone needing or having a passport in Pemba was remote. This had to be a hustle. The next morning Danji was feeding me mango through the door when the gentleman returned. His name was Mohammed. He revealed that he was the ambassador to Pemba sent from Dar es Salaam. Further he was the sole authority in Pemba, and I was in violation of immigration laws. He was shocked when I agreed, and he did not know how to respond to my confession. He sat there for several minutes considering his next move.

"Perhaps a payment of a fine will resolve this issue," Mohammed offered.

He was disheartened to learn that I had no money. We both knew that nothing great would come from my further incarceration. I told him that I was a capable person who could repay the community of Pemba with my skills. Mohammed smiled broadly and led me to a small thatched building across the town center. On the floor lay the town's generator scattered in pieces. Wete had not had electricity in several months.

By the third day I was family since all of Wete had come to know me. Danji and I were a great source of entertainment, and it was not uncommon to have more than forty onlookers surrounding us as we repaired the generator. The women brought us food, and the men observed in approval. Danji loved the work and the notoriety.

Nobody was more surprised than I was when the generator sputtered and then growled to life. We had been short on tools and parts. I spotted Mohammed in the crowd. He smiled, confirming that my debt had been paid. I was free to go but that potential left me with few options. Mohammed summoned me to his office and thanked me for my efforts. When he inquired about my intentions, I explained the events that had brought me to Pemba. I told him that I owed the old man's village a month's food for his assistance in getting us off of the reef. Mohammed remained silent for a few minutes and then stood up and walked to the door.

Yelling in Arabic, he assembled the entire town and told them of my dilemma.

Soon Wete was buzzing with everyone carrying food to Mohammed's office. Bags of rice, lentils, vegetables and fruits stood taller than Danji. Loading all the bags on bicycles, ten of us set off for the old man's village in the heat of the day. We all thrived in the effort, knowing that today we would leave more than we took.

The old man cried when he saw us. I walked up and touched his shoulder, confirming that I had kept my word. The people of his village gratefully accepted our gifts. Though only a few miles apart, we were all strangers yet somehow family. As was the way in Pemba, there was little use or need for words.

It took us three days to fill the Dhow with cloves. This was back breaking work that had not changed in a thousand years. My time in Wete taught me that I had gained little ground since Mexico. The cycle of life was impossible to avoid. I was back where I started. I had gone so far but changed so little. Everything has a method of survival and mine had not changed. I knew it never would.

A thick overcast set in that afternoon when Danji and I climbed on top of the mountain of cloves. Chasing the setting sun under a marmalade sky, we both lay on the cloves looking neither forward nor backward. I could not go home, for I was already there.

Searching my pockets I found the crumpled cloth note from Leva. I handed it to Danji. With a puzzled look he read, "You get what you give."

CPSIA information can be obtained at www.ICGtesting.com
Printed in the USA
270429BV00002B/2/P

9 780983 837206